Still
Procrastinating?

Still Procrastinating?

The No-Regrets Guide to Getting It Done

JOSEPH R. FERRARI, PhD

WILEY

John Wiley & Sons, Inc.

Published by John Wiley & Sons, Inc., Hoboken, New Jersey
Published simultaneously in Canada

Design by Forty-five Degree Design LLC

For general information about our other products and services, please contact our Customer Care Department within the United States at (800) 762–2974, outside the United States at (317) 572–3993 or fax (317) 572–4002.

Wiley also publishes its books in a variety of electronic formats. Some content that appears in print may not be available in electronic books. For more information about Wiley products, visit our web site at www.wiley.com.

Library of Congress Cataloging-in-Publication Data:

Ferrari, Joseph R.
  Still procrastinating : the no-regrets guide to getting it done / Joseph Ferrari.
    p. cm.
  Includes bibliographical references and index.
  ISBN 978-0-470-61158-6 (paper); ISBN 978-0-470-64289-4 (ebk);
  ISBN 978-0-470-64290-0 (ebk); ISBN 978-0-470-64291-7 (ebk)
  1. Procrastination. 2. Self-actualization (Psychology) I. Title.
  BF637.P76F472 2010
  155.2'32—dc22

                                                            2010013926

Printed in the United States of America

10 9 8 7 6 5 4 3 2 1

To all of the people who model nonprocrastination in life,
to my three children, Catherine, Christina, and Jonathan,
and above all my wife, Sharon, who models insight, patience,
and the best qualities in my life:
I dedicate this book.

Contents

Foreword
by
Timothy A. Pychyl, PhD

This book is long overdue. No, it's not a case of procrastination. Far from it. It's just that Dr. Ferrari, my dear colleague and friend, has been conducting procrastination research for decades. We've been waiting for him to write a popular book based on his research.

This is not Dr. Ferrari's first book about procrastination, however. In 1995, he co-authored an excellent scholarly book that summarized the research up to that date. It has been a must-read for any scholar interested in the topic. He has also co-edited two other scholarly volumes about procrastination since that time and more journal publications about the topic than any other scholar in the world.

Still Procrastinating? provides a summary of all of Dr. Ferrari's research written for everyone, not just those who specialize in psychology. Dr. Ferrari has integrated over twenty-five years of research into his own story about why we procrastinate and how we can learn to act differently.

As a scholar with an international reputation for his research, Dr. Ferrari has worked with academics throughout the world. He has collaborated with colleagues in Australia, South America, the Middle East, and Europe, as well as many others here in North America. And, true to his generosity of spirit, you will see frequent reference to the work of his colleagues and his students in this book.

It is important to recognize that you'll hear about Dr. Ferrari's students' and colleagues' research as well as his own, because this reveals something about the essence of the author. In addition to being a valued colleague, Dr. Ferrari is a caring and thoughtful mentor. He has guided many students at DePaul University directly through his work there, and he has mentored many junior colleagues throughout the world in their research. He is community minded, so it's not surprising that the other academic hat that he wears is in the community psychology program and as the editor of the *Journal of Prevention and Intervention in the Community.*

The scholarly community has publicly recognized Dr. Ferrari's outstanding contributions to the field. Among his many awards, this Vincent de Paul Distinguished professor has been made a fellow of the American Psychological Association and the Association for Psychological Science and a charter fellow of both the Eastern and Midwestern Psychological Associations. Most recently at DePaul University, he was honored with the Excellence in Public Service award. I see this book as another aspect of Dr. Ferrari's public service, an offering of his scholarship to the community at large.

I think this book is a good summary of what Dr. Ferrari has learned about procrastination. It reflects his understanding of this troublesome, self-defeating behavior in a way that allows readers to grasp the main issues identified in his research. Using everyday examples such as Christmas shopping, filing taxes, and simply getting to our most common tasks, Dr. Ferrari highlights how his research explains why we can become our own worst enemies.

In addition to his science, I think you'll get an understanding of the author himself. Dr. Ferrari takes the reader beyond the conclusions of his studies and offers his personal insight into how we might address this self-defeating behavior of needless task delay. This advice reflects a great deal of Dr. Ferrari's personal philosophy, his beliefs about the world, and what gives life meaning. In doing this, Dr. Ferrari creates a unique blend of science and personal philosophy that will be particularly appealing for those who share his spiritual perspective.

It is tempting to write more by way of introduction to this book and its author, but I think it's more important that you get on with your reading. As you'll see in the book, Joe and I agree on a very important basic principle about beating procrastination; that is, "just get started." Every journey begins with that important first step, and you're about to take that step as you read what this accomplished scholar has written about procrastination.

Timothy A. Pychyl, PhD, is an associate professor of psychology at Carleton University in Ottawa, Canada. He created the popular Web site procrastination.ca, which indexes all current and past scholarship and information on procrastination.

Acknowledgments

Writing this book was relatively easy. Writing these acknowledgments was a challenge. I am sure there are people I have inadvertently omitted, and I am sorry if you are one of them.

My interest in the study of procrastination began in the spring of 1985 sitting in a class taught by Dr. Rebecca Curtis of Adelphi University, in New York, called "Self-defeating Behaviors." I raised my hand and asked if procrastination as a self-handicapping strategy had ever been studied. Dr. Curtis said she could not remember for sure, but clearly it must have been done. I didn't stop there, and I found that there was no procrastination research in social-personality psychology, so this would be my focus for a dissertation. I followed the advice I once heard that one's dissertation could be placed well into the current mainstream of a discipline, or could be novel research to make one's career. I chose the latter.

A few small studies along the way led to the late Dr. C. R. Snyder of the University of Kansas phoning me in the early 1990s and saying, "Joe, it's time—it's time for you to write a book on procrastination and to make it the cornerstone of the field." He invited me to do an authored book for his social-clinical series, and I agreed. What a great mentor he was.

A few more studies later, Dr. Tim Pychyl of Carleton University, in Ottawa, invited me to come and speak to his graduate students as he began a research center for procrastination studies. The moment we met, after I stepped off the plane, we became friends. We collaborated on a special edition of a journal issue on procrastination that appeared in 2000. More studies later, that friendship-collaboration led to joining Drs. Henri Schouwenburg and Clarry Lay in an edited book on academic procrastination in 2004.

Along the way, there were keynote conference papers, invited presentations, and wonderful students to work with. I love the students at DePaul; they have taught me so much about research but, more important, about life. My career focuses mainly on undergraduate education, but I mentor masters students and a few doctoral students on procrastination research. Thank you to each of you for working so diligently with me: Christine Chandler, Joe Cohen, April Gonzalez, Corey Hammer, Jesse Harriott, Samantha Keane, Kim Mancina, and Emily Sumner. In addition, I want to thank Todd Bottom and Angela Koenigs for reviewing and editing this book prior to the final version. It is wonderful working with you both.

Among my colleagues, I thank those faculty from Elizabeth Seton College, Mohawk Valley Community College, Cazenovia College, and especially CUNY/Baruch College and DePaul University, who were supportive. Thanks to the chairs who granted time for procrastination research: Jerry Cleland, Shel Cotler, Chris Keys, and Walter Reichman. Colleagues who worked with me over the years need to be thanked, namely: Doris Argumedo, Russ Barone, Mike Berzonsky, Karem Diaz, Juan Diaz-Morales, Jack Dovidio, Leslie Eaton, Bob Emmons, Eva

Feindler, Judith Johnson, Bill McCown, Jean O'Callaghan, Mike Olivette, Bilge Ozer, Tim Pychyl Steve Scher, Henri Schouwenburg, Dianne Tice, and Ray Wolfe.

I thank Lucinda Rapp for providing moral support and teaching schedules to work on my scholarship. I am grateful to the staff at John Wiley & Sons, including Christel Winkler, my editor, for shepherding the book through contract and conclusion, and Lisa Burstiner, my production editor, for wonderful proofreading and editing. I am especially grateful to my agent, Cynthia Zigmund, for patiently helping me through the proposal and contract phases, as well as calming my jitters when I didn't think I could meet the word counts for Wiley.

There have been many family and friends who supported me and encouraged me to write this book. I am pleased they gently pushed me along.

And finally, I thank you, the reader, for having the courage to pick *this* book off the shelf and to read it. I hope and pray it brings you peace and meets your needs. You have taken the first step in stopping the habit of procrastinating: you admitted you wanted to learn how to stop. Congratulations! Now, take the next steps and finish your journey. I am humbled that I could be a source of comfort to you to enable you to stop.

Introduction

Why Do We Procrastinate?

On August 6, 2009, I returned from the 6th Biennial International Meeting on the Study and Treatment of Procrastination in Toronto, Canada. It's a two-day event in which speakers discuss how to treat procrastination in students and older adults. Yet a core group of us also attend to present our latest research from the previous two years or to provide serious issues for discussion and to suggest new directions in the field.

Don't laugh—no, it does not take us two years to organize the meeting. We use those two years to focus on collecting new data about the causes and consequences of procrastination and to analyze data on the cures. We meet every two years, in such places as London, Lima, the Netherlands, Toronto (twice), and even Columbus, Ohio.

As I walked through the airport terminal in Toronto on my way back to Chicago, I saw a series of billboards for the local bank, HSBC. The slogan printed on the billboards caught my attention and seemed appropriate for the beginning of this book: "The world would be a dull place if everyone agreed on everything."

I agree with that slogan. In this book, I try to capture the essential findings of the science of procrastination derived from the research I and others have engaged in over the last twenty years. You may not agree with what I say or with my views and suggestions. But often, as much as I can, I tried to link them to scientific studies conducted all over the world. As the billboard says, we all can't be the same because the world would be dull. In this book, I present some scientific facts that may not agree with what you believe.

What do we know about this complex tendency called procrastination? You may have heard the expression "the truth will set you free." In this book, I will provide you with information based on science. Notice that I do not say there is *proof*—something that is permanent, existing now, in the past, and in the future. Instead, I say the truth (with a small *t*)—the truth based on what we have learned about procrastination from scientific research during the last twenty years.

Information does help us grow and change; it gives us insight. But psychologists learned decades ago that insight alone does not cure. Merely knowing that the origins of your problems stem from your mother will not result in permanent change. It helps, but it's not sufficient. Consequently, in this book suggestions or strategies for change are provided wherever possible, and these strategies are based on your strengths. You see, you *can* change; however, *will* you change?

Perhaps my views on procrastination will seem controversial. They may upset you, maybe even arouse you. All I can say is that at least I got your attention. My goal is to enlighten you, inform you, and inspire you to change.

If you are a procrastinator, welcome to a new understanding of what you do—or don't do. If you are not a procrastinator, thanks for taking time to read this book. I hope you read all of it. You may choose to read only sections or chapters. That's okay. I tried to make them standalone chapters, yet I do link concepts across them.

No Standing, No Parking, No Waiting

If you've ever driven a car, been a passenger, or had someone come to pick you up, you've probably encountered a sidewalk sign with the words "No standing, no parking, no waiting." It's frustrating to see these signs when you try to pick someone up. Where do you go? How do you accomplish your task? The person you're picking up is waiting for you. The parking regulations are obstacles impeding your goal of picking up a friend or a relative. It is almost as if those signs are talking to the procrastinators of the world.

What certain procrastinators may not realize is that someone is waiting for them, and that person can't park, stand, or wait. There are things that have to be done, and they need to be done *now*. Procrastination is like stopping a train that left the station: when we procrastinate, we hold others up. We are telling the conductor, "Stop here, stop where I want you to stop" or even "I will get on that train when I want to get on that train." Eliminating procrastination from our lives is like trying to stop a moving train; it's not easy.

This book is more than a typical self-help approach for dealing with chronic procrastination. In fact, you should consider it to be of "mutual help" to you and all of the people you interact with. When you learn how to prevent the waiting, standing, or parking in your life, this will also benefit countless others whose schedules are delayed by your procrastination. I will show you how to

- *Stop waiting* for that perfect opportunity or time to act (it doesn't exist).
- *Stop standing* still and make the positive changes that will help you meet your needs and achieve your goals.
- *Stop parking* and missing all that life has to offer.

A recent radio ad playing in Chicago featured an announcer saying that he has written a poem about time: "Why does time have to fly? Why can't time walk? Stroll? Meander? Why fly?"

In reality, time is constant; it does not fly. There are 24 hours in a day, every day for 365 days a year (except during leap years, when we add another day). Time moves constantly. We can't simply say, "Time flies"; we must fly with it to take in all of the gusto and joy that life has to offer.

"Oh, no, another book on procrastination," you might be saying. Do we really need another guide on how to stop dawdling? Consider the following.

Every Christmas holiday season, I listen to version after version of "Jingle Bells" on my local "All Christmas music, all the time" station. It seems to never stop from Thanksgiving to Christmas Day. The song is sung by country and western singers and opera stars, recording artists from the thirties and forties to hip-hop and contemporary, both men and women, young and old, of varied races, non-Christians and Christians, instrumentals and vocals. All I can think is, How could there be a market for so many versions? Yet there is.

It's the same for procrastination. I Googled the word *procrastination* in book titles. Would you believe I ended up with more than 2,370 hits? Although *procrastination* was not in the title of every book, I was amazed at how many different books discussed the topic. Some of these were books on poetry, the classics, art, music, historical figures, obsessive-compulsive disorders, anger management, addictions (gambling, drugs, and alcohol), health prevention, hypnosis, deafness, women in the military, careers in nursing, coaching others, opening a fitness club—you name it. Even the Bible contains morality tales that caution against procrastination.

You probably think this will be another self-help book on time management, but it's not. Procrastination is a serious issue, with personal and societal consequences. Still, despite the impact of procrastination in our lives, we don't seem to take it seriously. Instead, we create annual weeks and months to focus on procrastination without really addressing the problem. Are you aware of the following unofficial observances?

- January is National Get Organized Month.
- The second week of March is National Procrastination Week.
- The third week of March is Clutter Awareness Week.
- September 6 is Fight Procrastination Day.
- October 24 is Take Back Your Time Day.

"Oh, you're just talking about the need for time-management training," you might be saying to yourself. Professors Brigitte Claessens, Wendi van Eerde, Christel Ruffe, and Robert Roe published a study in a 2007 issue of *Personnel Review* that looked at thirty-two empirical articles on time-management effectiveness from 1982 to 2004. Their results did not surprise procrastination researchers like me.

These scientists found that enhancing time-management training might improve time-management skills, but it does not transfer to better performance. In other words, if this book focused solely on time management as a solution to procrastination, as do so many other books on the market, you would still be a procrastinator when you finished reading it. You would find excuses for why the techniques sounded good but did not apply to your unique situation. Time-management skills do *not* help chronic procrastinators. Time management is nothing more than a Band-Aid.

It is time for you to stop making excuses. Start by substituting new thoughts and behaviors for those that prevent you from changing. Instead of saying, "I don't have the money," say, "I'm having a temporary cash-flow problem." You'll be amazed at what a difference it will make in your life! Commit to change. Many of the excuses we tell ourselves are rationalizations for procrastination in sheep's clothing.

Tardiness Is Tacky

Procrastination is so much more than simple tardiness. Gus is often late. He never anticipates traffic delays. He makes stops on his way to meet family members for dinner. The movie is starting and his friends are waiting for him, but Gus is still circling the parking lot. People get annoyed with Gus all of the time, but he always retorts, "I'm not doing it on purpose."

Being late for a beer with your buddies, even fifteen or twenty minutes late, may be a nonissue for the majority of people. But in most social situations, as well as in the workplace, tardiness is tacky. Using the excuse that your busy life makes you late is simply not acceptable. As you will see when you read this book, for most people punctuality is of the utmost importance and is critical to conducting business and building personal relationships.

Are you late because you are avoiding anxiety or anger or resisting something, possibly without realizing it? Maybe you are overscheduled, but why do you let yourself get consistently overextended? Procrastination is making you miss out on valuable experiences, opportunities for success, and quality time with family members and friends.

In this book, we'll explore the causes and consequences of procrastination. Procrastination is learned, so it can be unlearned. Major types of chronic procrastination have been scientifically supported and are covered in these chapters. I will also give you valuable tips on how these forms of procrastination link to social support, indecision, the work environment, academic performance, and a host of other factors. It is crucial that you understand *why* procrastination occurs. By obtaining accurate information based on scientific research, you can begin the process of conquering procrastination.

Who Is a Procrastinator—Especially a Chronic Procrastinator?

Trust me, what you are about to read is *not* a pop psychology "personality test" that you would find in a magazine. I can't offer you a diagnostic tool to determine whether you are a procrastinator in a pop quiz. Writers who try to do that, without scientific backing for the specific survey items they are offering, are misleading you.

As you will see, a sizable number of people procrastinate very often, almost compulsively. So, I wanted to offer you a chance to see whether you fit this profile. Again, this is not a reliable personality inventory, and these characteristics or attributes are not exhaustive. Chronic procrastinators possess many more characteristics than those I list here. Still, it is useful for you to examine whether you are prone to living this maladaptive lifestyle from moment to moment, situation to situation. Consider whether you have any or all of these characteristics:

- I am regularly late for meetings and appointments.
- I feel uncomfortable saying no to others when I'm asked to do something.
- I wait to meet deadlines until the last minute, because I get a kick out of beating the clock.
- I have lots of clutter around me and tend to be disorganized at work, at home, and in my life in general.
- It really is not my fault that I start and finish projects at the last minute, if at all; other people and other tasks that I have to do get in the way.
- I find it so hard to make decisions; I'm not a good decision maker.
- I know what I should be doing to meet deadlines, but I simply don't do it.

- It is so hard for me to just get started or to do more than one task at a time. It's easier if I don't even begin.
- I don't seem to be able to gauge how much time I'll need to get tasks done; I underestimate or overestimate what is necessary.
- It is difficult for me to organize things and then to get started, so I simply don't do it.
- I tend to focus on short-term, immediate pleasures, and I really don't think of or consider the long-term positive outcomes that would result from getting my tasks done.
- People know that I'm usually late in whatever I do (from purchasing gifts to getting sport or concert tickets). They know that I work hard and this is why I can't be punctual. If others pressure me to get tasks done by a certain deadline, I react by taking my time—they don't have the right to tell me when to do something!
- Life is short; I want to enjoy it *now*.

Do many of these attributes resonate with you? Did I hit a nerve? Or, perhaps it's not you whom these characteristics describe but instead your partner or spouse, your coworkers, or your friends. If these attributes are common in a person—I mean, *really* common—then I suspect that he or she is a chronic procrastinator, and this book is for that individual. Remember, this list is not a pop quiz. Instead, it describes a few issues and behaviors that might reflect your procrastination tendencies. I hope this book addresses your concerns and helps you learn to stop procrastinating. So, let's get going.

What This Book Has That Others Don't

After spending over twenty years focused on the topic of procrastination, I believe that not only do I know something about the topic, I know what is required to overcome it. You're probably saying to yourself, "You know about procrastination because you are a procrastinator." Actually, I'm not, but I've spent a good chunk of my professional life studying and interacting with procrastinators.

My familiarity with this topic is the result of trying to understand the causes and the consequences of procrastination through scientific research, not by casual observance. Colleagues consider me an international expert in analyzing scientific studies of procrastination. I'm the author of several scholarly books, as well as more than seventy professional research articles and two hundred invited keynote and scholarly conference presentations on procrastination, at the time of this writing. Individuals, schools, companies, and corporations rely on my knowledge and experience in solving procrastination-related problems.

I'm not bragging, but I assure you that I know what I'm talking about. In this book, I pool the knowledge, skills, and insights I've gained, which are all based on proven scientific techniques and strategies, to help you stop waiting, standing, and parking—in other words, to stop *procrastinating*.

This book will provide you with accurate, research-based information on procrastination that will help you live your life more fully. What makes this book different from others you may have seen or read is that it brings science to the forefront and separates speculation from superstition. Don't skip the main chapters and merely read what you think are the cheat sheets at the end of the book. You will not find time-management or quickie solutions. I don't take that approach. Instead, my goal is to demonstrate that time-management and street-corner solutions to procrastination will not work. This cognitive-behavioral problem is complex and has many intertwined roots.

Each chapter in the book is manageable but complete. The last thing chronic procrastinators want is long, drawn-out, belittling advice. They want to know what they can do—*now*—to get the task done. So, start reading, and always remember that many others are going through the same experience that you are.

Everyone Procrastinates, but Not Everyone Is a Procrastinator

Never put off till tomorrow what you
can do today.

—THOMAS JEFFERSON

———————

Never put off until tomorrow what you
can do the day after tomorrow.

—MARK TWAIN

The term *procrastination* comes from the Latin *procrasti-natus*, which literally means "forward tomorrow." If you always put off until tomorrow what you could—and should—do today, then you know that procrastination has a number of causes and consequences in your life and does not have a simple cure. Procrastination is a habit that you have learned and reinforced. Yet this habit can be broken. You *can* change it.

Of course, change will not occur overnight. Someone once said it takes twenty-one days to form a new habit. Another popular self-help author claimed that it takes on average, thirty days to make a habit. I'm not sure what science has determined in this regard, but if you've been a procrastinator for years, you will need many days to break this habit.

It's never too late to start, however. So, why do you procrastinate? Some people say it's because they have a fear of failure or a fear of success. Others claim that laziness is a reason—or is it really an excuse? Contributing factors for why people intentionally postpone tasks may be their lack of accountability for getting things done or their having various types of unrealistic expectations. Yet before we try to uncover the motives behind procrastination, let's focus on the definition of the problem.

In this book, you'll discover that breaking the procrastination habit will not be easily accomplished if you have a lifelong history of delaying and avoidance. Simplistic remedies won't work—for example, buying a timer, using a calendar, making lists, keeping a time log, creating an action plan, or merely becoming an early bird or a night owl. Instead, you need to realize why you indulge in this behavior, pinpoint when it occurs, and learn how to change it. I will review the causes and consequences of your habitual procrastination and, in the process, offer insights into the "cures."

This is not a typical self-help book on procrastination, in that I don't give you time-management strategies and say, "Now, do these things, and all will be well in your life." If you are a chronic procrastinator, you know that those suggestions won't cut it. They don't work. If you are a habitual procrastinator, you'll generate excuses for why such strategies don't apply to your life.

Defining Procrastination

In my scholarly 1995 text (Ferrari, Johnson, and McCown 1995), my co-researchers and I defined procrastination as "the purposive delay of the starting or completing a task to the point of subjective discomfort." Let me say this in more direct terms, with less technical jargon. People procrastinate—do not work on tasks—and, as a result, feel bad (anxiety, regret) from their delaying tactics.

Over time, however, some people seem to become comfortable with those negative emotions, and they continue with their decision not to act, even when it makes sense to act and is in their best interest to act. I must ask you now, "Why do you delay working on that project or making that decision? You'll feel better if you accomplish what you need to." Perhaps you don't know the answer, but in this book, I'll help you see the logic of getting started and completing the task. I'll provide information, backed up by scientific research, that yields strategies to help you overcome your tendency to procrastinate.

Yes, I've said it before and I'll say it again now: procrastination is negative—it is maladaptive. Recently, certain scholars claimed that some procrastination is adaptable, useful, functional; they say it is constructive and positive (e.g., Chou and Choi 2005; Choi and Moran 2009). They label such delay *active procrastination.* This term suggests that procrastination may lead to an overachieving person who works hard to produce the best product he or she can. I think this term is a misnomer and the expression of the concept is misdirected. Being active is procrastination? No, I don't think so. If you are working on another task rather than on what you are supposed to do, then you are avoiding what you need to do. So, you *are* procrastinating on the target task.

Watching TV so that you can avoid doing the dishes is not "active," in terms of getting the dishes clean. The dishes are not being washed, so you are procrastinating about dish washing. When there are no more clean dishes and you are eating with your bare hands and roaches are crawling out of the woodwork in your dirty kitchen, I don't view your procrastination as very adaptive.

Is procrastination the same as delaying or postponing? I will argue no (see chapter 7). Clearly, procrastination does have these time-related aspects. Delay and postponement are a part of procrastinating, yet they are not the same as procrastination. If one delays to gather more information or postpones a decision because he or she needs to do something important before the target act, then these strategies are *not* procrastination.

If you need to delay or postpone your behavior because of circumstances that are out of your control, that, too, is not procrastination. For instance, you may postpone taking a family vacation because there simply are not enough funds to pay for the trip. Is that procrastination? I would say no.

For an act to be considered procrastination, it needs to be a less optimal choice than getting a task done. It's irrational to procrastinate, because the delay or postponement is not the best choice you can make to ensure the success of the situation. Not washing clothes results in your having an empty closet; not paying bills contributes to your incurring a poor credit rating and possibly losing your home. Procrastination is not adaptive.

Dr. Piers Steel, of the University of Calgary, Canada, defines procrastination as "to voluntarily delay an intended course of action despite expecting to be worse off for the delay" (Steel 2007). Said another way, procrastination may be defined as "the voluntary, irrational postponement of an intended course of action despite the knowledge that this delay will come at a cost to or have negative effects on the individual" (Simpson and Pychyl 2009). These definitions are consistent with what I and my colleagues wrote about in 1995.

The process of delaying is voluntary or purposeful and deliberate. And the person feels uncomfortable, experiencing emotional unease from delaying, as we noted in 1995. Still, the person continues to delay—even when he or she feels bad about it.

Based on these two definitions supported by my research of the last twenty years, the delay makes you worse off—it's maladaptive. Procrastination, when it is your habit or is chronic behavior, becomes a maladaptive lifestyle. In this book, I will work with you to change that chronic tendency. It's not your "personality trait," something you are unable to change. Instead, I view it as a chronic behavioral pattern that needs to be changed and that you *can* change.

Dr. Steel's definition does include the idea that procrastination involves an irrational delay on an intended course of action, and he claims there is an element of impulsivity in procrastination. In chapter 12, I will discuss my research that suggests that procrastination "gone wild" is related to impulsivity, especially as a deadline looms.

The Role of Irrationality

Dr. Steel adds to the equation that people who intend to procrastinate and delay are making an irrational decision to not follow through and not finish what they want to do. In chapter 3, I detail the research I've done about the cognitive processes that are involved in procrastination, especially in regard to being indecisive.

If you are a procrastinator, the delay seems logical and justifiable. Listen to procrastinators—they may tell you their reasons, which sound quite appropriate, for not finishing what they wanted to do. But these are excuses, and they are irrational. In chapter 4, I describe my research on how these reasons turn into excuses for procrastinators to justify why they do not focus on a target behavior.

Why do people procrastinate when it is obviously irrational to delay? Throughout this book, I explore what I and others have discovered during the last twenty years:

- This maladaptive delaying is a way for people to self-sabotage their future performance by making them likely to fail (chapter 3).
- Procrastination is someone's failure to regulate aspects of herself or himself (chapter 3).
- Procrastination is irrational because it damages other people's perception of you (chapters 7 and 9).
- Procrastination does not lead to academic (chapter 10) or workplace success (chapter 11).

- Procrastination is irrational because it results in regrets and is an unhealthy form of rebellion against others (chapter 7).
- Procrastination does not promote a sense of perfectionism (chapter 4).
- In some cases, procrastination has implications for psychopathologies (chapter 12).

These consequences don't seem adaptive, do they? It's irrational for you to continue your lifestyle of procrastination, especially because you *can* change it, you *can* succeed.

"Mind the Gap": The Role of Intentions in Procrastination

In July 2005, my family and I traveled to London for the 4th Biennial International Meeting on the Study and Treatment of Procrastination, at Roehampton University in a local suburb. It was a great conference, and we loved seeing the city. I recall hearing the expression "mind the gap" over loudspeakers as subway trains pulled into a tube stop (as they call subway stations in England). As trains arrived, we were warned to step back from the edge of the platform and to be aware of the gap between the train and the platform. Sometimes, the warning referred to trains stopping at a slightly higher level than the platform. In those cases, we needed to step up into the train, perhaps three or four inches. We were being warned to "mind the gap" so that we wouldn't trip.

I think of that expression as an appropriate metaphor for procrastinators and the gap they have between their intentions to perform an act and actually performing the act. You see, we all intend to accomplish certain things, and psychologists have examined how those behavioral intentions predict whether we will actually perform the target acts.

The advice I must give procrastinators is to mind the gap—think of the gap between your intention to do something and then actually doing it. Why do you *intend* to delay your behaviors? The decision not to act now may be related to your intentions not to act. I'll explain how psychologists stress the role of intention in predicting behavior.

First, let me mention something called the *theory of reasoned action*, which was devised in the late 1970s and then expanded over the years by two psychology professors at the University of Illinois, Urbana-Champaign—Drs. Martin Fishbein and I. Ajzen (Ajzen and Fishbein 1977; Fishbein 1980; Ajzen 1991). I suggest that scholars who are interested in procrastination and mathematical models read their 1975 book, which is considered the definitive reference for the most popular expectancy-value formulation of attitudes, intention, and behavior.

According to this theory, which was proposed more than thirty years ago, attitudes are not a strong predictor of what people do, but they predict intention (abbreviated as BI, behavioral intent). Subsequently, BI is the best predictor of B (behavior), a much better predictor of an action than simply one's attitudes are.

For example, I like chocolate sweets but not candy bars. Give me cookies, cupcakes, and cake, but I am much less a fan of ice cream or chocolate bars. So, my attitude is strong on chocolate, and, given my waist size, it is apparent that I like chocolate a lot. Nevertheless, my behavior—whether I choose to eat that candy bar, especially if it's dark chocolate (too bitter)—occurs very infrequently. I don't like such forms of chocolate. If you want to think of this mathematically, I guess you could say that my BI to engage in the target behavior (eat chocolate) drops to 0 when I am presented with a candy bar.

So, BI is a good predictor of B, but it does not always mean that the person will perform the behavior, even if he or she values the act or sees it as worthwhile for others. If you are a procrastinator, remember to "mind the gap" between your BI and B.

Let me give you another example of how BI does not always predict B. In my research, an early area of interest was "blood donating." At some point in our lives 33 percent of us will need blood transfusions. But it has been noted that only 4 percent of us will be donors. We must tap into this resource (pardon the pun) of volunteers.

After my first master's thesis and then early in my doctoral program, I looked at ways to increase the altruistic act of blood donating. You can read the specifics of the studies referred to in the following paragraphs (e.g., Ferrari and Leippe 1994), but suffice it to say that we presented folks with persuasive messages that heightened their sense of moral obligation to help others and/or their need to help others in this important humanitarian way and that also lowered their fears associated with the act of giving blood (which is the most common reason that people don't give blood).

The participants' BIs were high, as were their positive attitudes toward the concept of blood donating, and many reported that they would attend the upcoming local blood drive. Yet when I went to record who actually attended the two-day event, few participants showed up. Even those who reported a strong BI to perform the act (donate blood) did not show up on either of the two blood drive days. The intent to perform the act was there (help others by donating blood), but actually performing the behavior (showing up to give blood at a local two-day drive) did not occur.

Fishbein and Ajzen's model has long been supported by empirical research (e.g., Ajzen and Fishbein 1977). Ajzen changed the name of the model to the "theory of planned behavior," suggesting that it is important to consider the extent to which people perceive control of their behavior. Later in this chapter, you will learn how the element of perceived control over a situation influences the likelihood to procrastinate. For now, that's enough of the social psychology lesson on attitudes, intent, and behavior. Let's return to procrastination.

To recap, psychologists believe that some people intend to do a task but don't fulfill their behavioral intention. In terms of procrastination, psychologists believe that people may also intend *not* to do a behavior. For these folks, a frequent, habitual, compulsive, chronic failure to fulfill their intentions seems to be a way of life—and it is maladaptive. Perhaps they forget to "mind the gap" between intentions and behaviors.

Let's go back to defining procrastination. For years, Dr. Clarry Lay, a retired psychology professor from York University in Toronto, Canada, has claimed that procrastination is a function of the BI-to-B gap (Lay 1986; Lay and Burns 1991). In short, procrastinators fail to move forward with their intentions (BIs). Procrastination becomes a more serious problem when the gap in time between hatching an intention and actually starting or finishing a certain behavior increases. Over time, the intention-behavior gap grows, from a few days to many days, and before the person knows it, *pow*: minutes turn into months.

Procrastination has transformed something that could have been done early and simply to a more intense and overwhelming challenge. "How can I ever accomplish this task and do it now?" procrastinators will say. "It's so late, it just won't matter," they might tell themselves. Or, "I would look so silly doing it now, because it's so overdue." Or the procrastinator may say, "Oh, this has gotten out of control, and I just can't handle it anymore." What was simple has become overwhelming. Researchers have shown that forming an intention that includes ways to implement your plan can result in nearly eight times more likelihood that you will follow through on your intention (Owens, Bowman, and Dill 2008). You must make a plan that includes the intention to do X and Y and then Z.

The task should have been started early, at the beginning of the intention. Remember, "Just do it—now!" The intention-to-behavior time gap even has societal implications. I recall when the AIDS and HIV epidemic was just starting to become a serious health warning. If our governments had devoted time, attention, and, specifically, economic resources when the problem began, it would not be a global epidemic now. One could say the same about global warming, the swine flu, and other issues.

Community psychologists call this *prevention*. I prefer to undertake prevention over procrastination. If we can handle our personal and social problems when they are small, we can prevent them from causing us a lifetime of grief and sorrow.

The longer the time between our intending to do a task and the deadline when we have to finish the task, the harder it seems for us to start. Dr. Lay's notions link well, then, to the theory of reasoned action from the 1970s (Fishbein and Ajzen 1975), which was restated in Dr. Steel's recent model (Steel 2007).

Dr. Lay recently placed *goals* within his definition of procrastination (Lay 2009). We all have goals we want to achieve. I say that you must make the goal of accomplishing a task more valuable than the goal of not working on a task. You need to make working on the task more salient (apparent) and highly desirable. Dr. Kennon Sheldon, of the University of Missouri–Columbia, has shown that we feel good when we make progress toward reaching our goals. As you get happier about reaching your goal, you motivate yourself to work even more (Schuck and Sheldon 2001; Sheldon 2004). It's a nice cycle that helps us get our tasks done.

It's also been suggested that procrastinators should do "intention updates" as they work on a task. As you work on a project, check in with yourself and ask, "How am I doing?" (in the words of former New York City mayor Ed Koch). Ask yourself whether you are any closer to the goal you intend to accomplish. What are you doing to stay on track? What will it take to get you back on track?

Sure, knowing your skills is important, but that may not be enough to reach a goal. Knowledge alone does not "cure." Regarding your goals, you need to ask yourself the following: What is reachable? What is unattainable? What can I do to reach them?

Identify specific, concrete goals. Make those goals behavioral. Look for specific things you can do. Can you write that legal brief completely, in one sitting? Not likely. But if you focus on one section at a time, you can do it.

Vague notions of goals such as "I have to clean the closet" will not be reached. Instead, say, "I will organize the shoe area in my closet by Tuesday, and then, for fifteen minutes, I will tackle the shirt section." By making the task manageable and giving yourself behavioral goals that are doable, you are more likely to follow through. Think of them as "minimally acceptable" goals, as clinical psychologists who study procrastination might say (Burka and Yuen 1983).

Certain procrastinators *intend* to do something but do not complete their intention. These people may say something like, "I never got around to it." I think this break in the procrastinators' intent-behavior relationship results in *regret*. They focus on the missed opportunities of their lives. They regret what they did not act on. They could have done it, but they chose not to do it. (See chapter 7 for details on regret.)

Why miss the joys and even the sorrows of life? When you are twenty years old, life may seem long because there appears to be so much more time ahead to engage in this or that. When you are eighty years old, life may seem short. In your old age, when you reflect on what you did and did not do, will you have more regret or will you savor the good times?

Chronic Procrastination: The Myth of "Working Best under Pressure"

I've heard a number of chronic procrastinators say that they procrastinate because it gives them a thrill. By working frantically to get things done at the last minute, they claim that they experience an adrenaline rush. For these "arousal procrastinators," waiting until the last minute might seem adaptive and functional, but I propose that they are wrong in their belief that they work best under pressure. Someone who claims to feel excited from trying to "beat the clock" as the deadline looms is mislabeling his or her feelings. We'll look at procrastination and such emotions in more detail in chapter 2.

Chronic Procrastination: Living with Fear and Avoiding Life's Pleasures

Some people procrastinate as a way to avoid certain outcomes and situations: this is called *avoidant procrastination*. It's when a person does not perform tasks because of fear: fear of things like failure, success, social isolation, or impostor tendencies. The avoidant procrastinator delays tasks because she is afraid.

I will not lie to you—you may fail at a task. A major league baseball player will strike out two out of three times when he is up at the plate. But he still goes up to the plate. He still tries. The person who visits Las Vegas or Atlantic City or any casino town may know that she will not strike it rich at the slot machines. But she continues to return to the casino, continues to try. An old campaign slogan for the New York State lottery was "You have to be in it to win it." Remember, you have to try in order to win; you have to get out of the boat if you want to walk on water. Failure may happen when you try, but nothing happens when you don't try.

Life is short—we have an obligation, a social responsibility, to try to make the earth a better place. As humans, we are supposed to help others. Readers with a Christian background will recall the parable of the three servants who were each given a different level of talents (5, 2, or 1). The first two servants doubled their returns with their talents, but the last servant simply buried his talents. A point of the story is that you need to use your skills to help others and not bury your talents.

The Fear of Failure That Results in Avoidant Procrastination

It is comfortable not to try something. It's understandable that fear may immobilize you. But this also makes it very likely that you will miss out on many important things.

Let me share a personal story. A few years ago, my wife and I celebrated our twentieth wedding anniversary. I decided to take her on a surprise trip to Lake Tahoe, a place we both had always wanted to visit. I planned several adventure jaunts for us to experience, such as Jet Skiing, kayaking, riding mountain bikes, and parasailing. I am not the most comfortable person when high up in the air, especially when all that prevents me from crashing to earth is one rope, as is the case with parasailing. But this was something my wife had always wanted to experience. And it was important that we soar through the air together. Was I afraid? You bet! I gripped my hands tightly onto the safety ropes until my knuckles turned white. I tried not to look down. This was pure fear. But it was important not to delay, not to create excuses, not to let fear override the joy on my wife's face as she looked out over the lake and toward the mountains.

Procrastination would have kept me in my comfort zone, but then I would have missed out on one of the joys in life. If I avoided and put off the sky ride to another day, that future day might not have come.

Two summers later, my wife and I spent a few days at Universal Studios in Florida. At the Islands of Adventure theme park, the first ride we hopped on was the Hulk, which is considered one of the wildest roller coasters out there. Although I was still filled with trepidation regarding such thrill rides, I moved forward in dealing with experiences that were "out of my comfort zone." There can't be any procrastination in conquering one's fears, even if they are conquered in small steps. Fears keep us from challenges and keep us comfortable, but they also prevent us from enjoying life. Life is not easy, even though "some assembly is required." But what a great life it'll be!

Still, people will wait. We prefer to use expressions like "killing time" or "wasting time." But you have not touched time. You need to stop avoiding tasks and missing out on the joys of life.

Let me give you a little background information from the field of psychology. In 1983, two clinical psychologists from California, Drs. Jane Burka and Lenore Yuen, published a popular self-help book called *Procrastination: Why You Do It and What to Do about It*. Based on their observation of clients, they claimed that fear of failure was a cause of procrastination (Burka and Yuen 1983). In 1984, Professors Laura Solomon and Esther Rothblum of the University of Vermont published a paper showing that many students delayed important academic tasks (studying, registering for classes, writing) because of fear of failure (Solomon and Rothblum 1984).

On the other hand, in 1992, Professor Henri Schouwenberg, now retired from the University of Groningen in the Netherlands, reported that fear of failure may cause some students to procrastinate on academic tasks, but not all procrastinators have this motive (Schouwenberg 1992). He found that only high (chronic) procrastinators experienced a fear of failure. In 2007, after conducting a meta-analysis of the literature on procrastination, Dr. Piers Steel of the University of Calgary found a small correlation, or relationship, between the fear of failure and procrastination. He concluded that fear of failure will cause some people to procrastinate, but that same fear will cause others *not* to procrastinate (Steel 2007).

So, in 2009, Dr. Timothy Pychyl and graduate students Mohsen Haghbin and Adam McCaffrey, all from Carleton University, presented a study examining the role of fear of failure in procrastination (Haghbin, McCaffrey, and Pychyl 2009). They demonstrated that fear of failure for procrastinators is multidimensional. That is, some people may procrastinate because they're afraid of feeling shame about being inadequate. Other people procrastinate out of a fear that a poor performance or a failure may result in the devaluing of their self-esteem. Still other people procrastinate because they fear that failure would upset others who are important to them.

Pychyl and colleagues showed that the fear of failure that may motivate procrastination is mediated by a person's need satisfaction. In other words, if people think their needs are not going to be met, then they will procrastinate. If they feel incompetent and as if they have little control over the outcome of a situation, this may cause them to procrastinate. To put it another way, fear of failure results in procrastination when a person believes she has "low competence"—that is, little ability to do something—and low autonomy in controlling the setting (psychologists call these factors two components of the satisfaction of our needs). When these needs are not met, a person will procrastinate.

Hang in there a little longer, if you are following all of this. Why should you try to do something when you don't think you can do it well? Why even try when you feel you have no control over the situation? Heck, you might as well procrastinate.

Back in the late 1970s, Dr. Martin Seligman, from Pennsylvania State University, reported on a series of studies with dogs that changed the way psychologists conceived of depression (Seligman 1975). I won't give you all of the details, but Dr. Seligman placed each dog in a harness suspended slightly off the floor. They received a mild but annoying electric shock to their left hind paws. (Note that the pain was not something that permanently maimed or harmed the dogs, and no dog was killed.) The dogs never knew when the shock would be delivered (it was unpredictable), and they could do nothing about avoiding the shock (it was uncontrollable). Later, when these dogs were given an opportunity to escape or avoid shock while in a different situation, the dogs merely sat in the corner and "took" the shock. Dr. Seligman called it *learned helplessness*. The dogs learned to be helpless after experiencing a series of uncontrollable and unpredictable unpleasant events.

How is this related to procrastination? Some procrastinators may feel the same way that those dogs felt. Is a feeling of learned helplessness holding *you* back? Even when you want to change, you think you can't. Life, in your opinion, has given you uncontrollable situations, with unpredictable outcomes. The fear of failure you experience contributes to your procrastination because you believe you have low competence—you don't have the skills to deal with change. And you feel that you have no control over your life; your life and your time are controlled by the demands of others. So, you procrastinate.

I want to help you realize that you *do* have control; you *do* have the skills to change. Now you need to cultivate the desire to change. You're reading this book, right? That tells me you have the willpower to change. In this book, I want to give you the *way* power: the skills you need to change. According to psychologist Dr. C. R. Snyder from the University of Kansas, a person with both willpower and waypower has a sense of hope about the future (Snyder 1984). If you are a procrastinator, I will give you hope about your ability to change.

Procrastination: Everyone Is *Not* Doing It

"Later," "tomorrow," and my favorite, as a parent of teenage kids, "in a second" are phrases we hear so often from procrastinators.

Before I offer you ways to deal with procrastination, in a blend of science with self-help advice, let me address the issue of how global procrastination is. You may wonder, How many people really are habitual procrastinators? The answer is simple: it's very widespread. Still, keep in mind that everyone procrastinates, but not everyone is a procrastinator.

Every one of us, at some time or another, has delayed the start or the completion of a task. That's normal; that's life. For instance, you may have a multitude of things to do, so you write up a priority list. Clearly, items written later on the list are delayed so that you can complete those with higher priority. Are you procrastinating? No.

There is undoubtedly a task or activity that you simply don't enjoy and keep putting off. Does that make you a procrastinator? No. You may not get to work on that task often and may delay it, but eventually the task will be completed. That's normal, a very adaptive way to get things done. As I noted earlier and expand later in this book, *delay* is not procrastination; *waiting* is not procrastination.

For example, Rob does not enjoy mowing and trimming his lawn. It is not a very large yard, but during the spring, summer, and fall months it needs to be cut. Folks who have a lawn will tell you that they spend money and time to fertilize it, weed it, and water it, only to cut it and repeat the process over and over. For some of you, the repetitive task is doing the dishes or washing clothes. If you put off doing this task until it can't be avoided any longer, does that make you a procrastinator? Again, no.

The actress Patty Duke had a series of hits throughout her life. She won an Oscar for her role as Helen Keller in the 1959 film version of the Broadway play *The Miracle Worker*. She even won praise from critics and the public for her role in the 1960s TV series *The Patty Duke Show*, in which she played identical cousins who laughed alike, walked alike and, at times, even talked alike. Yet Patty Duke stated, "It was forty years of procrastination," when she was asked why she had not returned to Broadway production until the 2000 revival of *Oklahoma*.

The citizens of Australia have an expression—"Gunnado," meaning, "I'm gonna do it." We have become a global society where delaying tasks is accepted and widespread.

What are you waiting for? Why not include more of the Latin expression *carpe diem* (seize the day) in your life? Dr. Timothy Pychyl, a research psychologist from Carleton University in Ottawa, Canada, has done some important studies on procrastination. His blog through *Psychology Today* gets thousands of hits. He has a cartoon series on his "Procrastination Research Group" Web site (www .procrastination.ca)called "Carpe Diem." The famous Nike ad says, "Just do it!" Dr. Pychyl is fond of saying "Just get started!"

Get started, if only to work on little pieces of your task. Procrastinators like to put things off for the future, for when they are "in the right mood." "Just start!" is what I would say.

Make a draft of the paper you need to complete; take down just two of those kitchen cabinets for remodeling. Get started, so that you don't feel overwhelmed. It doesn't work simply to tell some people, "Just do it," because they look at the entire task and say, "I can't." If you do some of the chore, there will be less remaining, and it will gradually get done.

John Ortberg, a pastor and a teacher, wrote a motivational-spiritual book that espouses the need to get involved in life: *If You Want to Walk on Water, You've Got to Get Out of the Boat.* If you want to experience all that life has to offer, you must become engaged in it. You must get out of the boat, take the risk of getting wet, and start it now.

A chronic procrastinator never moves down that to-do list. She may finish one or two tasks but keeps writing the list over and over, reshuffling things and focusing on the list instead of on the tasks. Procrastinators generate a number of tasks that are avoided over and over. They always have a great reason for the delay. We will talk more about blame and excuse making later on, but suffice it to say that procrastinators repeatedly delay tasks—a large number of tasks—usually with plausible, believable "reasons."

Procrastinators live in the now, so there is no tomorrow. There's nothing wrong with enjoying the moment—it's healthy and constructive. But it becomes destructive and dysfunctional when one does not also plan for the future. We don't know whether we will have the time and energy tomorrow to accomplish the goals we need to achieve.

I once read that the Muslim faith does not support procrastination. The prophet Muhammad called on Muslims to take the initiative to do good deeds before any problems arose. He said, "Lose no time to do good deeds before you are caught up by calamities awaiting you." These calamities might include starvation (which may impair your wisdom), prosperity (which might mislead you), old age (which could damage your senses), or even sudden death.

These are good words to live by, regardless of one's religious preference or level of spirituality. In fact, St. Vincent de Paul, the patron Roman Catholic saint for the university I work with, is paraphrased as saying, "Do, and then do more." There are too many good deeds that need to be done in life, and we must do them. By doing good deeds, we become virtuous, and our hearts grow with love for others.

If we combine the words of these two religious leaders, we see that procrastination is not only personally maladaptive, it is nonconstructive to others. Procrastination may help you for a moment, but it does not help others who may need your actions to accomplish their goals or who may need your assistance.

Studies indicate that 70 to 75 percent of college students admit that they engage in procrastination for tasks such as studying, registering for classes, completing reading assignments, or keeping appointments with professors. In fact, 70 percent of doctoral students do not complete their dissertations—they stay in the unofficial title of A.B.D. ("all but dissertation"). And that title is B.A.D.

As you will see in the next section of this chapter, about 20 percent of average adults (both men and women) report that they procrastinate as a lifestyle. The 20 percent of adults who identify themselves as procrastinators actually engage in this maladaptive lifestyle. They delay as a way of life. Although many of us might not enjoy completing specific tasks or may feel overwhelmed by having too many chores and duties, the *chronic procrastinator* is someone who very rarely—if ever—starts or finishes tasks on time.

Does the rate of procrastination, then, decrease as we get older? No. We are talking about two different (but related) patterns. The college student may delay studying and reading but does not delay getting free pizza in the dorm or free tickets to the hip-hop concert in the quad for the first fifty attendees. *Everyone procrastinates, but not everyone is a procrastinator.*

The Prevalence of Procrastination in the United States

I conducted a number of studies derived from survey data collected from many public speaking engagements across the United States. Attendees reported on various demographic items, such as their age, sex, marital status, education level, employment status, and job title.

In addition, attendees at these speaking engagements completed procrastination surveys that were short and simple (remember, procrastinators don't have time for anything too involved). They filled out Leon Mann's (1982) five-item Decisional Procrastination (DP) scale, Clarry Lay's twenty-item General Procrastination (GP) scale, and Bill McCown and Judith Johnson's (1989) fifteen-item Adult Inventory of Procrastination (AIP). If you are interested in the actual survey questions, refer to the 1995 book by me, Johnson, and McCown (cf. Ferrari 1989).

In one study we conducted (Harriott and Ferrari 1996), participants included bank employees, professionals, business employees from several companies, and members of the general public. Our results showed that about 20 percent of the men and the women (no significant gender difference) identified themselves as procrastinators, a rather high prevalence among regular people. In fact, it's higher than the rate for clinical depression.

In a subsequent study we conducted (Hammer and Ferrari 2002), participants were white-collar employees from the Northeast and Midwest regions of the United States. These respondents included business professionals, education specialists, and a miscellaneous assortment of other professionals (doctors, teachers, and lawyers). Again, the rate of chronic procrastination was around 20 percent for both men and women.

We conducted yet another procrastination study (Ferrari, Dovosko, and Joseph 2005) based on data collected across the United States from consulting work with a major food distribution company. Company sites were located in major U.S. cities (New York, Tampa, Dallas/Ft. Worth, Las Vegas, and Seattle). We tabulated the rates of procrastination of sales employees and midlevel managers, plus a sample of noncorporate white-collar workers, and also compared rates from various U.S. regions: the Northeast, the Southwest, the Northwest, and the Southwest. The Results? Again, 20 percent of adult women and men reported themselves as chronic procrastinators.

Where do people who delay filing their federal taxes most likely live? Following is a table showing the top five cities in the United States for 2008 and 2009, according to Turbo Tax. Did you notice that these cities generally stay in the same top slots and merely switch positions? Procrastinators love to delay, and they live all over the country.

Top Five Cities for Tax Procrastination

2008	2009
Chicago, IL	San Francisco, CA
New York City, NY	Houston, TX
Houston, TX	New York City, NY
Austin, TX	Chicago, IL
San Francisco, CA	San Diego, CA

Rates of self-identified chronic procrastinators again were around 20 percent for both men and women. In fact, we found that for chronic procrastination, male and female corporate employees reported significantly higher rates than did non-corporate white-collar employees. Moreover, among the male and female business professionals, sales employees had higher rates of procrastination than did midlevel managers, and procrastination rates were higher in the Northwest than in other parts of the United States. In all three studies, the results were the same: about 20 percent.

One in five adults is like you, in that he or she engages in frequent procrastination. This fact is important because it shows that thousands of people are procrastinators, and you need not feel as if you are alone or different from others. No blame needs to be assigned. Your tendencies to delay are learned habits that many others also express. You now need to *unlearn* them.

The International Prevalence of Chronic Procrastination

I once read a story about a U.S. academic who taught classes in Germany while on sabbatical. Germany, to my mind, is one of those countries where precision and productivity are exacting.

I would not expect procrastination to be a common occurrence within the German culture. Well, this professor reported that when he taught a graduate class at 6 p.m., every student arrived late the first night. The lateness continued on the second night and even on the third. Students were not showing up until 6:10 or 6:15 each evening.

In frustration, on the third evening the professor asked why students did not show up on time for class. A student in the front row, rather seriously, asked, "You mean around 6:15?" Confused and with an irritation that bordered on anger, the professor requested clarification, because the start time was clearly stated as 6 p.m. in all scheduled announcements.

It seems that in Germany, academic systems rely on the "quarter hour," so a 6 p.m. class will start at 6:15 p.m. It is expected that students will show up late and the last person to enter the room will be the professor. If one wants to start at the listed time for a class or a meeting, the listed time would need the suffix "s. t." (*sine tempore*, or without extra time), over the usual start at 15 minutes after the stated time, or "c.t." (*cum tempore*, or with extra time). If the suffix is not added, a 6 p.m. start time is really a 6:15 p.m. start time. The Germans figured out a way to make being late something that should mean being on time.

My son's high school band director has an expression I like that you might have heard before: "To be early is to be on time, to be on time is to be late." I try never to be late (e.g., I leave my house at 5:15 a.m. for an 8 a.m. class, and it is only a thirty-five-minute ride from home to campus—but you never know how bad the traffic will be, which could prevent you from getting to Chicago).

How prevalent, then, is chronic procrastination around the world? I wanted to know, so I partnered with colleagues from other countries to investigate this issue. I could have simply placed procrastination measures online and let people who visit a Web site complete the procrastination scales. That would have been easy. But not everyone in every country (especially certain underdeveloped countries) has access to a computer. And if people do have access, their time online may be limited. I think it is safe to say that conducting procrastination research using only online methods would give one a biased sample of more affluent, better-educated, and possibly younger participants. My international colleagues and I would have gotten a very biased sample if we had restricted our studies only to people with Internet access. Therefore, we went at it the "old-fashioned" way: we surveyed adults living in these countries.

We conducted prevalence studies from men and women of the United Kingdom, Australia, and the United States. Across all three countries, the rates of chronic procrastination, for men and for women, were—you guessed it— about 20 percent (Ferrari, O'Callaghan, and Newbegin 2005).

In a follow-up study, we gathered more international prevalence rates of procrastination among 1,600 adult men and women. Based on one scale in the study, the prevalence of procrastination was about 14 percent, and based on the other scale, about 15 percent—for both men and women. That totals around 29 percent of adults.

Do you need more convincing that chronic procrastination is widespread? In yet another study with adults living in Turkey, we found similar rates. Consistent with the previously mentioned studies, 20 percent of adults identified themselves as chronic procrastinators (Ferrari, Ozer, and Demir 2009).

When I visited Saudi Arabia in January 2009 for an invited address on public health practices, I expected the meetings with officials to start late. The tour books stated that in the Saudi culture, people did not begin meetings on time, following a custom that everyone expects the leader of the meeting to be late. To my surprise, all of the meetings—at the university and in the government—began on time and ended within the meeting times.

Dr. Humood Al-Sherif, from King Saud University in Saudi Arabia, and I examined the prevalence of arousal and avoidant procrastination among more than a thousand adult men and women living in that Middle Eastern country. What did we find? You guessed it: a 20 percent prevalence of procrastination.

So, what does all of this mean? It means that although everyone procrastinates, it seems that about one-fifth of men and women—at least, those living in the United States, the United Kingdom, Australia, Spain, Peru, Venezuela, and Turkey (and we know of folks who did similar surveys in the Czech Republic, Poland, and Austria)—may be labeled chronic procrastinators, either arousal or avoidant. In other words, *you are not alone.*

Prevalence Rates Based on Gender, Age, Marital Status, and Education Level

I want to explore one more point to show that you are not alone. You may wonder whether that 20 percent rate breaks down differently for men and women; for younger and older adults; for single, married, or divorced adults; and for people with different educational degrees.

The gender myth. During the last twenty years, I have heard a common refrain that one gender is more likely to procrastinate than the other is. When I talk to women's groups, they tell me that the description of the typical procrastinator sounds like their husbands, like the men in their lives. In contrast, when I talk to men at public presentations, they say, "That describes my wife—she's the procrastinator!"

The truth is, both men and women make up the 20 percent statistic. Research studies indicate that there seems to be *no significant gender difference* in procrastination. Don't be fooled by people claiming a gender difference based on very small statistical yet not meaningful differences. Both men and women report the same rates in the United States, as well as in other countries that were surveyed. I want you to be aware of this fact, because the media keep telling us that men—or women—are more likely to be procrastinators, that it's a Mars versus Venus thing. Many people hold this false belief. There is no meaningful difference between the sexes, at least when it comes to procrastination. Millions of people are procrastinators, all of whom are not getting the most out of life.

The age myth. It has been said that adults in their twenties procrastinate more than people in their fifties do. I've examined the prevalence rates by age and again found no significant difference between young and older adults in tendencies to procrastinate, which was also corroborated by my colleagues in international samples. Now, if we examine the very elderly, we might find that older citizens move more slowly and perform tasks at a different speed than active younger adults do. But this difference is developmental—as we age, we slow down and become less active. Nevertheless, there is no need to stigmatize any generation as being more likely to procrastinate. It's simply *not true.*

The marital myth. You may wonder whether marriage helps or hinders procrastination. Studies show many benefits in health, happiness, and longevity for individuals who are married. Still, I haven't found any consistent pattern in procrastination rates for married versus single versus divorced versus widowed individuals. We cannot use being married or single as a predictor of who will or won't be a procrastinator.

A spouse, as the common saying goes, may "drive you to drink," but he or she does not "drive you to procrastinate."

The education myth. Is someone with a high school education (or less) more likely to procrastinate than a person with a bachelor's or graduate degree? Simply stated, no. There were no significant differences in procrastination rates between the highly educated and the less educated, among the international samples we obtained. We cannot blame education—or the lack of it—as a reason for procrastination.

The absent-minded professor is no more likely than the high school dropout to be a procrastinator. We even examined the characteristics of frequent procrastination among adult Spanish men and women. Regardless of age, gender, marital status, and education, chronic procrastination was prevalent at similar levels among all international samples of adults.

Yet even though misery may love company, that's no reason to stay in the same boat with other procrastinators. The rest of this book will show you how to understand the causes and consequences of this very prevalent lifestyle. After all, if you can't understand why you procrastinate, there's no way you can change. I want to help you learn to change. You can do it, and you can do it *now*.

I wrote this book in a format that will help you learn from experiences that enable and empower you. Let's get started. Say to yourself, "I will not wait anymore: no more gunnado—get it dun!"

"I'm Better under Pressure": The Arousal Procrastinator Myth

Procrastination is like a credit card: it's a lot of
fun until you get the bill.

—CHRISTOPHER PARKER

———————————

I love deadlines. I like the whooshing sound
they make as they fly by.

—DOUGLAS ADAMS

The Thrill-Seeker as Procrastinator

A widely held misconception by some procrastinators is the belief that they work best under pressure. Russ tells everyone he is a thrill-seeking junkie who needs to wait until the last minute to do anything, whether at home, at work, at school, or in relationships. It's not uncommon for Russ to begin writing papers at midnight that are due the next day. But is Russ successful using this last-minute strategy?

I work best under pressure is a familiar refrain, but it's simply not true. My research does not support this perception. Most likely, Russ is wasting time by not getting started. He would be more productive if he focused on what he needs to do now. Procrastinators like Russ believe they need that extra jumpstart—just before a deadline—to work effectively. They believe that being under time pressure motivates them.

Reporters frequently ask to interview me for stories they are writing about procrastination. They say they have a "story deadline" in one or two days and must get the information from our interview immediately. They tell me that last-minute, need-to-rush procrastinators are common in their newsrooms.

During the summer of 2009, I corresponded with a reporter named John, who worked for a major London newspaper. He said I could include his story in this book.

"On Monday I pitch about a half-dozen ideas, briefly summarized, in an e-mail to my editor in London," John said. "The editor of my section will take what he likes into a big meeting with the twelve heads of rival departments on Tuesday. Like dogs, they tear each other's ideas to pieces to make their own ideas shinier: 'I read that before.' 'That is boring.' 'Who cares about that one?'

"This Darwinian winnowing carries on every morning until Friday, when a final decision is made about what may appear on the pages—about fourteen stories being sifted from Monday's initial fifty stories by nine writers. And then we start to write our stories. Procrastination is built into the system.

"What a system! Instead of letting the best stories emerge, competition forces writers to wait until there is little time for the story to appear that Sunday. If anything, people who procrastinate leave little room for error. On the other hand, shopping early for a dinner party allows them enough time to look elsewhere for better produce and matching napkins."

I often hear high school and college students state that they have a paper or a research project due, often the next day. Frankly, it's unlikely that an instructor would have asked students to write a major honor's thesis or a term paper or conduct a research project in only a few days. I suspect that these students are procrastinating, just like the reporters. In both cases, the procrastinator will say, "I work best under a limited time frame."

Chronic procrastinators who live on the edge and race against time might think that they are arousal procrastinators who succeed at their tasks—but they don't. Psychologist M. Zuckerman, from the University of Delaware, coined the term *sensation seeking* for people who race against the clock to experience a thrill. These people believe they need an adrenaline rush, which they claim comes from working under a tight deadline.

My colleagues and I have conducted research that suggests that procrastinators are easily bored and distracted (Ferrari 1992c, 2000; Ferrari and Diaz-Morales 2007a). Many people believe that the motive for their procrastination stems from a need to increase arousal and reduce their proneness to boredom. They rush to avoid feeling bored. Yet one wonders whether they are actually rushing to avoid something (if so, their procrastination is motivated by thrill-seeking) or whether, after they rush, they label their heightened excitement a thrill (in this case, their procrastination results in a thrill). In psychology, we are asking the question of whether the thrill is the antecedent or the consequence.

I'll give you a concrete example of what I mean. The quarterly marketing report for your boss is due on Friday, and you were asked to manage this project about three weeks ago. But right now it's only Monday afternoon. In fact, this week your child has a school concert on Tuesday evening, your sister asked you to take a day trip to the casino on Wednesday, which you've been planning for months, and Thursday is your important conference call with the main office. So, there are lots of reasons you can't start today, now, on this project—right?

Besides all of these "reasons," you have always found that you *work best under pressure* when you have little time to meet a deadline. You know from the past that you like to work on these assignments the day before they're due. "Keep it close to deadline" is your motto.

So, you continue your weekly work, take Wednesday off, and engage in that conference call on Thursday. Now it's 3:30 p.m. Thursday, and you have a chance to have coffee with a coworker, who has just returned from a wonderful vacation to the same spot you and your family were thinking of visiting next month. You want to hear all of the details. What do you do? Go and listen to the stories, see his photos, and ask for details about the trip? Or do you start to write the report, with only a few hours left until the deadline?

Procrastination motivated by arousal suggests that you need the thrill and will start to generate excuses ("reasons," you might call them) for not beginning the marketing report on Thursday afternoon. If you tell yourself those excuses and even say, "Yes, I work best under pressure," and if you remember other times when waiting until the last minute really got your "juices flowing," as you excitedly came up with new strategies only hours before the deadline, then you call yourself an *arousal procrastinator*.

Yet procrastinators simply don't do well under time limitations. Procrastinators make more errors and complete less of a task than nonprocrastinators do when there is a time limit. Procrastinators under various time-limited conditions make more errors and complete fewer of a task's components than nonprocrastinators do, even though procrastinators believe they perform as well as others. Procrastinators can't seem to regulate their time and talents to do more than one task, so they put off completing a task to the point that they can't complete it accurately.

In other words, I suspect that it is not arousal that causes you to procrastinate. Arousal is not the preceding event before your procrastination. Procrastination, as I defined it in chapter 1, is never adaptive or successful. You may be delaying a task, but you are not procrastinating. You may be waiting, but that is not procrastination.

Instead, I suspect that you fool yourself into thinking that you need this last-minute rush. You repeatedly put off working on a task until you are close to its deadline because you fool yourself into thinking that this is the best way for you to work. Any emotional satisfaction that you experience from delaying is not what motivates you to continue to delay. Instead, the "thrill" sensation you are experiencing is anxiety for rushing at the end with little time left; the emotion is a consequence of your delay, not a cause.

And telling others, such as me, a researcher conducting studies on procrastination, that you *work best under pressure* sounds like a plausible, believable, and quite common excuse. It's a socially acceptable statement to tell people and maybe yourself. As I have shown in a number of studies, as a procrastinator you are concerned about what others think of you. So, why not give them a socially acceptable reason (excuse) for why you wait to complete tasks?

Christmas Shopping and the Procrastinator

Let's consider a real-world deadline that affects many of us: Christmas holiday shopping. A National Retail Federation survey found that shoppers completed less of their holiday shopping by a certain time in 2008 than at the same time in 2007 and that 41 million U.S. shoppers had not yet even started.

Sure, you've heard all of the ads that say waiting until the last minute to buy an airline ticket may save you money. Travelers who wait often claim that they get great opportunities to purchase lower-priced plane tickets. Once again, procrastination pays, creating the cliché "delay can pay."

Every year, on December 25, people around the world know that they have a deadline to complete all of their preparations— from decorating to gift shopping to food preparation—in order to be ready for the Christmas holiday. Yet every year, the same people wait until the last minute to shop and prepare. They run around buying gifts for family and friends, selecting from the already-picked-over merchandise in stores. They purchase a tree and food items for the next day, settling for what is left on the shelves. And they complain about it.

Many of these procrastinators report that they don't want to repeat the frenzy of last-minute shopping next year. Is it only unrealistic planning that causes procrastinators to procrastinate? Other procrastinators say that they love the experience and really enjoy running around to get everything done by the next day. The latter call the emotional upheaval they experience from last-minute shopping a "thrill." Is that you?

In a field study that I conducted with holiday shoppers (Ferrari 1993), on every weekend from the Friday after Thanksgiving until Christmas Eve, holiday shoppers indicated their style of procrastination and their reasons for shopping that day. The location was a typical U.S. mall, with 4 major department stores, one at each end of an X, plus 120 other shops. Approximately fifty thousand shoppers were there each weekend, according to the mall's executive personnel. Each weekend a random set of shoppers completed the questionnaire on measures of procrastination that was discussed in chapter 1 and rated a list of reasons for shopping at this time, as opposed to some other day that season. Participants received a three-dollar mall gift certificate that expired in six months. (Stay with me on this one—there's a reason the amount is only three dollars.)

Results showed, not surprisingly, that as December 25 approached, scores on the procrastination survey increased: more procrastinators waited to shop near Christmas Eve, rather than doing their shopping earlier. Some procrastinators claimed that they waited because they enjoyed shopping at the last minute—it gave them a rush. The various excuses given by procrastinators for why they were shopping so late came down to the fact that they blamed work and family commitments, not themselves, for the last-minute frenzy.

Watch out for those excuses! In this 1993 study, I showed that procrastinators are great excuse makers. You can come up with a plausible excuse quite easily, but there is one problem: the excuse prevents you from doing the task and reaching your goals. Whether you are tired, hungry, or under the weather, you need to assess whether this is a reason or (again) an excuse.

If you give yourself a reason that you can't finish a chore or even start it, then use that excuse to trigger an intention to start. Even if you limit the amount of time you spend on the target task, let the idea of the excuse be your signal to begin. After all, in fifteen minutes you can clean most of a small bathroom or sort through a couple of medium-size boxes.

Yet something puzzling also occurred in the 1993 Christmas study. About 30 percent of those small gift certificates were never cashed. Remember, they were good at all four large department stores and at the other 120 shops; they were redeemable for six months after they were given out, so people could use them for after-Christmas sales, Valentine's Day, President's Day, January white sales, Mother's Day, and Father's Day. True, the coupon was worth only three dollars, but it was still free money. Which 30 percent of shoppers didn't cash in their coupons? They were procrastinators. All of the nonprocrastinating participants cashed in their gift certificates. Yet procrastinators did not; they procrastinated until it was too late.

You don't need to rush at the last minute to accomplish your tasks. In fact, you may find the shelves empty, the stores out of the product you want, and the pickings pretty slim. Consequently, you may settle for a gift or an item that is not what your loved one really wants. The gift will most likely be returned. You've wasted your time and the gift recipient's time.

Don't blame the "season as the reason." Everyone knows that Christmas falls on December 25 every year, and the dates for Hanukkah are determined well in advance, even though they vary each year. Many people plan ahead and start their shopping early. Some people even shop all year long, purchasing gifts they come across that they know their family or friends will enjoy. Others make a game out of it.

In fact, it's possible that the shoppers in this study who didn't redeem the certificates simply lost them among all of the items they were carrying as they rushed from store to store. They might not have understood that this three-dollars-off certificate was good for any store on that day or at any store during the next six months. As a result, the certificate was not redeemed.

The positive emotional satisfaction you experience after shopping at the last minute could be turned into an even more positive feeling. Imagine how good you would feel knowing that you have finished your shopping one or several weeks before the holiday. Try it. Get your shopping done by the first of December. Then focus on enjoying the season—the lights, the decorations, the parties, the festive time of the year. Shopping early allows you enough time to look around for better gifts or fancier holiday napkins and dishes and food.

In fact, if you shop early, you can still go shopping on December 24, but this time for fun and not because you have to. If you see something small for a family member or a friend, you can take time to think about it and consider whether the person would enjoy the item. You won't need to buy it simply to have a gift to give. This new item would be in addition to whatever you've already purchased. What a different experience this type of shopping would be! As a bonus, you can stop for a coffee and watch everyone else run around the mall in a panic. Your shopping was finished weeks ago. What a great feeling!

In summary, you don't need to wait until the last minute to get things done. Do you want to feel good? Then complete a task when you have time to do it. You'll experience the thrill of finishing early. Do you find shopping unpleasant? Make it more attractive so that you finish it before the deadline. Then celebrate! The next time you accomplish a task early, such as filing your taxes before April 15, plan a party with friends. That should make you feel good.

Living in the Moment with Drop-Dead Deadlines

Many procrastinators are poor at estimating the amount of time that's necessary to complete a task, and they differ from nonprocrastinators in their time orientation. Procrastinators are oriented toward the present. They don't focus on what will happen in the future or on upcoming tasks. Instead, they focus on the past or the present.

Of course, it's sometimes good to be "in the moment." It is also adaptive to focus on what will be so that we can plan ahead. There are many tasks in life, such as holiday shopping, that require us to be systematic and plan for what will happen. I am not suggesting that you become anxious or worry about the future. That doesn't help anyone. Yet being aware and mindful of what needs to occur is an effective way to live and helps you conquer your tendencies to procrastinate.

I don't care much for the expression "a drop-dead deadline." I can figure out the deadline part, but I have to ask, "Who is doing the dropping? Who is going to die?" If you think about it, this is an insulting expression. People use it when they are asking others whether the results of a task really, truly have to be submitted by that due date.

Does that mean that the person who initially set a specific deadline has lied about the actual due date? I doubt that. A deadline means a deadline—it is due at that time. Don't insult others by asking when someone really wants something; assume that the person told you the first time.

Separate your emotions from the task. It's not necessary for your everyday tasks—paying bills, cleaning out the garage, cutting the lawn—to stir up negative emotions in you. Paying a bill is kind of neutral. This act does not have to reflect your self-worth or your character as a person (Burka and Yuen 1983).

There seems to be a general feeling in the United States that cheating at deadlines—that is, trying to get things done at the last minute, even when you know the deadline never varies—is a fun thing to do. Consider April 15 and the act of filing your taxes. Every working adult knows that federal income taxes are due on April 15. So, why wait until 11 p.m. that evening to mail your tax returns? In Lawrence, Kansas, there is an annual tax party at the main post office where last-minute filers are honored with cheers and streamers for filing just before the building closes. This is wrong. Instead, we should have a party for those who file on February 15 or March 15. Don't reward people for being late! Give the worm back to the early bird.

Why do we celebrate procrastination? Why do we reinforce living on the edge and fulfilling our responsibilities only at the last minute? Instead, we ought to focus on meeting the initial deadline. That might involve our paying attention to the future, to what we need to do next, while also being mindful of the moment. Focusing on the past is fine, as long as you don't become anxious and ruminate about past failures (Cohen and Ferrari 2008). Focus on what you can do now and what you need to do next.

In Buddhist traditions, focusing on "the now" is called being *mindful*. Going with the current and staying in the present are aspects of mindfulness. Don't dwell on the past or on your failures. You can't change the past. Maybe you performed poorly on a certain assignment. That happens. Remember, you are human. You will occasionally make mistakes, but you can learn from your past mistakes. You can gain control by staying in the present. Focus on what you can do now and what you will do in the future. Learn from the past; don't let past regrets ruin the present.

Evolution and Procrastination: What Is the Survival Value of Irrational, Intentional Delay?

I'd like to end this chapter about procrastinators' need for thrills with a brief comment on evolutionary psychology. You may not agree with Darwin's theory of evolution, and that is fine. I won't try to convince you of its validity. It is not relevant to your understanding of, and attempt to deal with, procrastination. Yet I'll give you a simple explanation of how current evolutionary psychology might view the value of procrastination toward keeping you, your family, your relatives, and your species alive.

Dr. David M. Buss, of the University of Texas, Austin, states that much of the behavior we engage in has some adaptive value that keeps us as a species alive (Buss 2009). Buss views personality traits as forms of strategy that people have adopted to ensure their survival. Thus, we need to identify the strategies (traits) that allow us to thrive and those that cause us to falter in various environments. Only members of a species who have skills that enable them to survive and propagate will continue their bloodlines.

DePaul graduate student April Gonzales claims that procrastination was useful for the human race in prehistoric times. There was limited food available for our ancestors, so humans ate and enjoyed themselves immediately, whenever they had the opportunity. Who knew whether there would be food later today, tomorrow, or next week? How could people know if they would live to see tomorrow or next week? There was no point in worrying whether others liked you in your new animal skin clothing, especially if you didn't have food right now. Consequently, humans were impulsive and did whatever made them happy for the moment. They had a "carpe diem" mind-set.

We could argue that procrastination during caveman times was an adaptive behavior and lifestyle. There was no need to worry, plan, or even consider the future. Humans had immediate life-sustaining needs to take care of. But we are no longer cave people. We don't need to live impulsively or believe that we perform best when we have limited time to complete a task. Our brains have expanded, and our lives are more complex. Ms. Gonzales would say that we should drop this caveman strategy of procrastination. Instead, let's look for more adaptive ways to live today. We've evolved; let's move forward.

Procrastination and Health

To recap, some procrastinators believe they work best under pressure. They feel that this motivates them and that they do their best work when trying to beat a deadline. This is a common, yet false, belief, because procrastinators seem unable to accurately assess their performance and to judge whether an outcome is successful. This was proved in lab experiments and real-world situations such as the study on Christmas shopping (see also Simpson and Pychyl 2009). Procrastinators estimate time by focusing on the now more than on the future. They ask for "true" deadlines, in the belief that the initial time frame given must only be an estimate.

You need to accept the fact that you have deadlines and you must meet them. There is no point in creating unnecessary stress by putting off tasks and procrastinating. For years, scientists and medical doctors have reported that constant elevated levels of stress hormones in the body negatively affect the metabolism, making people feel tired and lethargic, and preventing their immune systems from functioning effectively, which makes them susceptible to illness and disease. Procrastination is literally not good for one's health (e.g., Tice and Baumeister 1997).

Studies have shown that only 25 percent of people who begin exercise programs will be following them two months later. Where are the other 75 percent? Here come the excuses— a lack of time (but they can watch the latest TV reality show when it airs three nights a week), they don't like exercise (but they can sit for hours in front of a computer screen), they can't afford a gym membership (but they have money for that double-espresso latte every morning), and the list goes on.

Professor Fuschia Sirois, from the University of Windsor, Canada, has done wonderful research on the effects of procrastination on people's health (see Sirois, Melia-Gordon, and Pychyl 2003; Sirois 2004, 2007, 2009). The bottom line—it isn't healthy! From headaches, body aches, colds, and the flu to more severe cases of tooth decay, stress, and strokes, people who live a lifestyle of procrastination are sick more often than those who don't, and this results in health complications.

Do *you* do this to yourself? If so, develop a plan to complete each task. Break the activity down into small parts, do something you enjoy, find a trainer, exercise with family and friends, and reward yourself for each time you exercise.

Don't fool yourself into thinking that you perform best at the "eleventh hour." You don't. Tasks you could do now but keep putting off will contribute to your stress levels. The unfinished business will lurk in the back of your mind all day, adding to, instead of eliminating, your stress. You must do the vital tasks that you hate but need to do. Do them now. It will free you up to focus on more enjoyable activities.

Sit down tonight and plan for tomorrow: where do you need to be and when? What chores do you need to take care of? Prepare food to take with you tomorrow. If you resolve to exercise, stick to your plan.

Live in the present, and don't focus on the past. And don't think that you work well under pressure. If I asked you to generate a list of all of the times you performed successfully by waiting until the last minute to complete a task, and then I asked for a similar list of all of the times you failed or asked for extensions or completed most, but not all, of the assignment, I suspect that the failure list would be longer than the success list. In fact, if you could think of the dates of those successes and failures, I'd also bet that your successes from waiting until the last minute to do something were not very recent. You are probably focusing on past accomplishments from many years ago.

Let them go—let go of those past events and focus on the now and on the future. These are the time lines you can control.

Just because other people wait until the last minute to perform a task (such as holiday preparations) doesn't mean it's the right way to do it. Remember what your mother used to say? "If [insert friend's name here] jumped off a bridge, would you jump off, too?" Listen to your mom.

Imagine what you would feel like this year if your holiday shopping was finished by December 1; if your income taxes were filed by March 15 (unless you have to write out a check, in which case you would certainly wait until it's closer to April 15); if your summer travel plans were arranged by May; if your registration for college was completed by June instead of September; and if your monthly mortgage payments were paid two months in advance. Just imagine. Now make those feelings a reality.

Indecision: Decisional Procrastination

In a moment of decision, the best thing you
can do is the right thing to do. The worst
thing you can do is nothing.

—THEODORE ROOSEVELT

———————

Nothing is so exhausting as indecision,
and nothing so futile.

—BERTRAND RUSSELL

To be, or not to be. That is the question." William Shakespeare's tragic character Hamlet did not know what to do: "Do I kill my stepdad, my uncle who murdered my real dad and married my mother, or do I let him live?" Many psychiatrists see the story of Hamlet as a prime example of human indecision, the turmoil we experience in life over the choices we must make. Do I decide to act? Do I decide *not* to act? Or, do I decide *not* to decide?

In chapter 1, we explored the role of intention in the process of procrastination. People decide not to perform a task, or, to put it another way, they decide to procrastinate. There is an intention to withhold the action. Do we act, or do we not act? Whatever the reason for the behavior, there is a delay. Make no mistake, however—putting off a decision *is* making a decision. There is an intention not to act.

Life is a process of transitions. We make transitions from childhood to adolescence, and from younger to older adulthood. Growth and making decisions are part of our everyday lives while we are engaged in making transitions. We make minor decisions: what to wear today, what to eat for dinner. We make more mid-level decisions: Do we take a family vacation this year? Where will we go for vacation? And we make major, life-altering decisions: whom to marry, which job to take. Should we move to a new house in a new city? The point is, we are creatures who have choices and we make decisions on how to live with our choices.

Saving for retirement is a common act that many folks avoid and delay doing. In such cases, there is an intention *not* to save for retirement. The person has decided not to save. Of course, people have many reasons for not saving now for future retirement. For instance, they say they don't have the money or don't make a good enough salary to put something aside for retirement. Others say they need the money now, for basic essentials.

These may all be good reasons. But ask yourself, are they instead more excuses for not saving? Do you have money to take that trip to Atlantic City or Las Vegas? Do you have funds for weekly lottery tickets? Do you buy yourself an extra-tall espresso coffee every morning or a case of beer each week? Do you have to own the latest cell phone or MP3 player that's available, with the newest "improvements," every six to eight months? Don't tell the procrastinator that his or her reason is an excuse; that person doesn't want to hear it.

So, why do some people delay in making decisions? Why do they live in a state of indecision? You may have heard the old expression "The road to hell is paved with good intentions." Is it simply that our busy lives prevent us from getting around to doing the things we plan or intend to do? Sometimes, this may be the case. The problem arises, however, when we have the ability to make decisions and choices and we don't do it. We delay, we put it off. Indecision is a very common form of delay. Maybe you wish the decision will go away. Or you hope that others will make the decision for you. Perhaps you don't have the personal resources or skills to make an informed decision.

Research and clinical professionals consider indecision to be *decisional procrastination.* Psychologist Leon Mann, from the Melbourne University School of Business, said that indecision is a dysfunctional decision-making coping strategy.

As U.S. president Teddy Roosevelt said, it is worse not to make a decision than to make a decision that is incorrect.

One may wonder whether decisional procrastination (DP) is related to a lack of competitiveness or time urgency. Barbara Effert, an undergraduate at SUNY Institute of Technology, and I examined the relationship between DP and time urgency and competitiveness (Effert and Ferrari 1989). We found with a sample of more than a hundred adults that DP—indecision— was not laziness. Indecisives report that they are similar to decisives in being competitive and they can work effectively.

Still, one wonders how quickly and efficiently indecisives and decisives work on tasks—whether they trade off speed for accuracy. Dr. Jack Dovidio, now at Yale University, and I explored the speed and accuracy of both indecisives and decisives (Ferrari and Dovidio 1997). We asked them to sort a deck of cards into black or red piles and then to repeat the sorting of cards into one of the four suits (hearts, diamonds, clubs, and spades), recording their speed at finishing the tasks and the number of errors made with each sort. We also asked indecisives and decisives to press a button as fast as possible whenever a white light appeared. After one hundred trials at this task, the participants were then asked to press the same button if the light was white but not press it if the light was red.

That is, indecisives now had to make a decision (like Hamlet)—to either act or not act. Both decisives and indecisives were equally fast, and there were not large differences in the accuracy of their performance. It seems that on simple tasks (such as sorting cards or responding to a visual light), indecisives are able to make quick, yet effective, decisions.

Indecision is not a lack of ability to make decisions quickly— indecisives choose to be slow. They seem to be easily distracted and they daydream, which is what I found in a study conducted with DePaul graduate student Jesse Harriott and Dr. Dovidio

(Harriott, Ferrari, and Dovidio 1996). Indecisives have the ability to focus clearly and can choose to make a decision. This is an important point you need to hear again: If you are an indecisive, it is crucial for you to realize that you are not lazy. You *can* make decisions, and those decisions can be effective.

Perhaps you think you are immortal. Why decide now? Why not decide tomorrow or the next day or next week? Because there will always be a tomorrow. Overestimating how much time you have to complete a task is dangerous, in that it gives you an illusion of immortality. "Why rush? I'm young. There is plenty of time to (invest, marry, have children, etc.). I'll make that decision right after I do X or Y." The truth is, there is only a limited amount of time between the cradle and the grave, and delaying those major life decisions may be an ultimately painful way that you avoid facing your mortality. I realize that making major decisions is not easy or fun, but it is essential in life.

We all make mistakes and errors of judgment. Fears of failure are ever present and never pleasant. No one wants to fall flat on his or her face, and many people (those "glass is half empty" types) are quick to remind you that you might make a mistake in your decision. Not reaching your goals and failing to decide how to proceed also makes you publicly vulnerable. Others can see your failures. Remember what President Teddy Roosevelt said—it's better to make a decision that is wrong than not to decide at all. And to that sentiment, we can add William Shakespeare's famous quote "It's better to have loved and lost than never to have loved at all."

You have to be *in* the game of life to *win* the game of life. Only by trying do we succeed. Inertia will not result in a fulfilling life. Risks and gambles are part of living. What I am asking is that you make informed decisions and choices, to increase the chances of your success in life.

Here is a social situation you may find familiar. Sally and her old friend Alice decide to go to the local multiplex theater that shows thirty-one different movies. They stand by the ticket booth, and Sally asks Alice, "What do you want to see?" Alice responds, "I don't care; you decide." Sally says, "No, I decided the last time, you pick the movie." Alice states, "I don't care, I don't know." Sally responds, "Come on, it's getting late; the movies start in three minutes." Alice again says, "I don't know; I can't decide." So, Sally picks the movie. They pay for the tickets and enter the theater.

Now, by not deciding what they should do, Alice creates an interesting situation: If the movie is enjoyable, they both leave the theater happy and content. If the movie is not enjoyable and not what they expected, Alice can turn to her friend Sally and say, "Why did you make me spend all of that money for that movie?" If the movie is a dud, Alice can walk away without her self-esteem or social image harmed. After all, she did not pick the movie. In either case, Alice, by being indecisive, comes across looking good. In both cases, the decision is not hers, so she can bask in the glory of a positive decision or distance herself from a poor decision by Sally.

Yet life is full of choices and decisions. Alice expects Sally to make decisions for both of them and doesn't play an active part in the decision-making process. Alice is giving up her right to express her choice. In fact, it seems inappropriate for Alice to complain if the movie is something they did not enjoy. Sally had to make a decision, and the choice was handed over to her by Alice.

Keep this in mind if you let others make choices for you. Life involves making choices, and being able to decide what one wants is part of being human. Human decision making has become a science in psychology and neuroscience. Understanding the processes and the products of decisions has implications. Clearly, we must exercise our skills to make decisions.

Dr. Michael Berzonsky of SUNY Cortland and I examined the decision-making processes reported by a couple of groups of indecisives and decisives (Berzonsky and Ferrari 1996). Dr. Berzonsky is an adolescent-development psychologist and has explored the processes of identity development. One style of identity that some adolescents, and even many adults, adopt is a *diffuse identity*. People who have a diffuse identity avoid self-exploration. They try not to learn about their strengths or their weaknesses. They fail to commit themselves to any personal life values and understanding of who they are. Their style of identity is unformed; it is diffuse.

While some people are interested in learning more about themselves (being what developmental psychologists call information oriented), other individuals are diffuse. Diffuse identity might be considered a form of "escaping from the self" (see Baumeister 1991). These people, in trying to avoid knowing themselves, seem to be escaping certain aspects of themselves. Studies have shown that procrastinators have a diffuse identity (Berzonsky and Ferrari 1996, 2008).

Dr. Berzonsky and I found that decisives want to know what they are good and not so good at doing. Indecisives, however, prefer to avoid learning more about their strengths and weaknesses in various skills. If you are an indecisive, you have the ability to choose. Challenge those irrational thoughts that make you decide not to act. Try keeping a daily journal. Many things that we tell ourselves to put off doing sometimes are really not connected with the task. Instead, they are related to the feelings we have about doing the task or about the outcome if we finish the task. Keep a journal—write down your thoughts and then challenge them. What is the worst that could happen if you finish a certain task? It's adaptive and constructive for you to know your strengths and weaknesses. If you avoid making decisions and knowing who you are, you cannot live your life to the fullest.

Making a decision is a challenge and something that we all need to do. You've got to get out of the boat if you want to walk on water—you need to take a chance if you want to enjoy life. As I mentioned earlier, you can at least make simple choices in life. Decision making is a skill we naturally possess as humans.

Multithinking: Complex Choices with Many Possibilities

Now, it's possible that some people intend not to act, or decide to procrastinate, for less obvious reasons. Certain people may experience receiving too much information from too many sources—something that might be called "information overload."

How do indecisives (decisional procrastinators) handle the lack of control over various situations in their lives? How do they make decisions when they do move forward with action plans? How do they search their resources to make informed decisions? What about major, complex decisions, especially those that involve conflicting choices and competing demands? For example, how effective are you at making a decision while also considering other things at the same time (something like multithinking, which is similar to multitasking)?

Are you unable to purchase an item because you can't choose among several alternatives? For example, Ralph often buys two lamps because he doesn't know which one he likes more. He brings them home and then, maybe, decides on the one lamp that best fits his family room redesign. Now, does Ralph return the one he does not want? Or does he hold on to the receipt—misplace it in a pile—and then after thirty or sixty days go to the store to try to get a refund? The customer service representatives at many stores would say, "Sorry, our return policy is valid for only a specific amount of time." So, Ralph is stuck with two items (plus all of the time and energy he spent and the cost of extra gas when he tried to return the unwanted item).

Many indecisives say this scenario sounds familiar. Are you one of them? You find yourself unable to decide which shirt to buy, which rug to order, which book to check out. As a consequence, you buy three shirts, order two rugs, and check out several books from the library. Then you fail to return the shirts, lose the receipt to the rugs, and pay overdue fines for the books.

It is possible that indecisives, compared to decisives, search through information differently when they make decisions, especially if the amount of information is exceedingly large. Dr. Dovidio and I explored this in a couple of experiments with sample groups of indecisives and decisives (Ferrari and Dovidio 2000, 2001). As the amount of information increased, indecisives searched through less information initially and then searched through more information on the item they chose but not on those they did not choose. In contrast, decisives wanted to know about the items they did not choose, as well as about the one they chose. Decisives tried to garner as much information as they could before making a choice, whereas the indecisives avoided information gathering.

Consider this situation. You (the indecisive) and your friend Sam are shopping for a new car and are considering a Honda, a Toyota, a Subaru, a Volvo, and a Hyundai. Both you and Sam choose the Toyota, and at first, you both read as much about that car as possible (e.g., resale value, maintenance history, optional equipment). But this is where you stop. As the number of choices for a new car increase, you search less information. Sam, the decisive, reads as much as he can about each of the other cars. Why?

It's not that indecisives simply can't process a lot of information; they can. Instead, we believe that indecisives *choose* not to handle lots of information. They are easily distracted and avoid absorbing as much information as possible whenever they need to make a decision.

Again, this approach is not adaptive. We recommend that people learn as much as they need to make a decision. You must discover alternatives before making a simple or complex decision. If a manager never decides which direction the office will go, then no one in the office will succeed, and the company cannot advance. The business succeeds when a choice, albeit an informed choice, is made.

Self-Regulation and Decision Making

Another way to consider the differences between indecisives and decisives is to explore their ability to effectively self-regulate. Self-regulation, which we'll discuss in chapter 4, is the ability to monitor various life processes at the same time. Will indecisives be able to regulate their speed and accuracy when performing a task? That is, can they efficiently use the limited amount of time they have to complete a task, while maintaining a high level of accuracy in their performance?

Studies have shown that indecisives can effectively balance good performance speed with accuracy. Again, as with simple and more complex tasks, indecisives are able to make effective decisions (Ferrari and Dovidio 1997). So, don't say to yourself or others, "I can't decide." Instead, say, "I am choosing to decide. I can make a decision, and although it may not always be correct, I choose to decide."

Researchers have learned that making frequent decisions may take a toll on indecisives, more than it does on decisives.

That is, after making a certain number of decisions, indecisives cannot make a set of additional decisions. (Decisives, however, are not similarly affected by making numerous decisions.) Dr. Tim Pychyl, from Carleton University in Ottawa, Canada, and I examined the decisional fatigue effects of indecisives and decisives in a series of experiments (Ferrari and Pychyl 2007). Participants had to make more than nine hundred snap decisions. Then they were asked to make a separate decision on whether to act or not act. It seems that after engaging in many rapid-decision tasks, indecisives become cognitively "fatigued." In fact, indecisives even reported that they knew they were fatigued! Apparently, because they didn't make decisions often, they had not used their decision-making "muscle" enough, and it was simply out of shape. The key here is to practice making simple decisions and then progress to making more complex decisions—build your multithinking strength. Just as an athlete or someone training for a marathon does, you need to get your multithinking muscle in shape by frequently making decisions.

How Does Indecisiveness Develop?

Where does this tendency to delay making decisions come from? One's genes? One's upbringing? There are no known genes that would influence a person to delay making decisions, but studies have shown that indecisives, like other types of procrastinators, had interesting home lives while growing up. Many indecisives (decisional procrastinators) had mothers who were indecisive and fathers who were very cold and demanding. Dr. Michale Olivette from Syracuse University in New York and I examined the parental upbringing of indecisives and decisives in a couple of survey studies

(Ferrari and Olivette 1993, 1994). The home lives of indecisives were rather dysfunctional. Consider the situation—the father was impersonal and demanding; the child couldn't rebel openly because the father would become even more unreasonable, so the child learned to procrastinate and be indecisive. The child couldn't turn to mom for help, because she tended to be indecisive as well.

It is also true, however, that in this same household, one sibling may have grown up to be a procrastinator and the other a nonprocrastinator. How could this happen? Because one child learned that procrastination was adaptive for him or her at the time. Later in life, procrastination tendencies continued to serve that person successfully. The other sibling learned to deal with life challenges directly and head on. Given that these two were siblings, it shows that procrastination is not genetic but learned. Is there hope for the procrastinating sibling? Of course! As researchers say, if it is learned, it can be unlearned.

I am not suggesting that you blame your indecision on your parents. It does no good to assign blame or to imply that you can't change because your parents made you that way. Instead, you should focus on changing and on making decisions: start with the simple ones and move on to more complex choices.

Focus on Success, Not on Potential Doom

The lessons derived from our studies, taken altogether, demonstrate that as an indecisive—a *decisional procrastinator*—you seem to have learned this strategy as a coping technique while growing up. You found that if you avoided taking in too much information before you made a decision, it was adaptive: it had some benefit for you. Perhaps by being indecisive, you managed to protect yourself from perceived and actual psychological threats. Now, as an indecisive, you may be choosing not to gather all of the information you need to make an informed decision. Instead, you prematurely cut off the fact-finding process. Occasionally, that might work. Yet most of the time, having all of the information before you make a choice or a decision works best.

If you are frequently indecisive, you need to modify this lifestyle. What happened in your past can't be changed. It may have been unfortunate, but it doesn't have to hinder your future. You are able to make decisions and don't have to rely on others to make them for you. Sure, some decisions, but not all, will be wrong. Many decisions you make will result in success. Don't stay in your comfort zone. Enlarge your boundaries and abilities. All of us are capable of doing or being more. Make the decision to improve. Focus on the successes, and forget the failures.

Moreover, you must practice making simple decisions so that your decision-making ability does not get fatigued. Think of your decision-making skill as a muscle—the more you use it, the more tired it becomes. Yet over time, the muscle will get stronger. With more practice, you will enhance your ability to make effective decisions. Making decisions, like riding a bike or learning to drive a car, is a skill that is learned with practice.

How to Make Better Decisions

We all struggle with making decisions, from the right investments to choosing a new career path or deciding which refrigerator to purchase. If you use the right approach, however, the tough calls may be a little easier. Here are a few simple suggestions:

- *Limit your options.* The research I did with Dr. Dovidio on how indecisives and decisives search for information before they make a decision offers us hope. Avoid "choice overload" by grouping your options into shared characteristics. If you're thinking of changing a job, categorize the jobs into "full time" or "part time." Then, ask yourself whether you want something sedentary, like a desk job, or you'd rather keep moving and be active. Continue categorizing until you narrow down your options.
- *Journal your thoughts.* Write down any thoughts you have that prevent you from acting. Then challenge those that are irrational and unproductive. So what if you fail? At least you tried.
- *Do the math.* Make a list of pros and cons. If you are torn between moving to a smaller apartment in the heart of the city or a larger place on the outskirts, make a list. Add the values of the items you list on each side, and see which side is longer. Be sure to consider the value you place on each pro or con (e.g., you might need a new car soon to drive into the city, even if your suburban home does have all of the space and the amenities you desire).
- *Don't look back.* Once you decide on something, move forward. My great uncle immigrated to the United States from Italy. Once, when I was a child, I asked him whether he longed to return to "the old country" where he had been born. He told me, "I only look forward, not back." After you've committed to a choice, have no regrets. Move on, move forward.

- *Take your time.* Be careful here—take time to decide, don't take time to stall. You need to make a decision, but only after you have collected important pieces of information. Yet you don't need *all* of the information because more will always arise. Take the middle ground. Whereas going with your gut is not always the best plan, gaining information to make a decision is the most adaptive and functional way to act.

Navigating Phase 2 of Your Life

Life, especially when we are adults, seems to have two major phases. In the first phase, perhaps during young adulthood, we seem consumed with establishing our careers, creating a marriage and a family, building a home to live in, and enhancing our friendships. These are all important aspects of life, to be sure.

But this "phase 1" of adulthood seems to be controlled by external forces. We are concerned with the opinions of others and how they may judge us through our jobs, our life partners and children, our homes and their décor, and the size and depth of our best friend relationships. We monitor how others perceive us. Our decisions seem focused on what others like and think.

Yet there comes a time in our later adult years, call it "phase 2," when we make a transition and turn more inward. At that time, we see that it is important to help others, to give to others, and to understand that other people are important in our lives. Building community relationships and participating in social activism and civic engagement seem important. Perhaps at this point in their lives, many people become more spiritual and active in their faith communities.

When your life undergoes this transition, whatever helped you reach your goals in phase 1 might prevent you from attaining them in phase 2. The skills you needed to succeed during your early adult years might be a hindrance in actualizing your later adulthood years. You need to make a decision to let go and learn new ways of living.

Sometimes, failure is the best thing that can happen to us. Failure moves us, helps us transition to the next level of life. Failure may lead to a personal conversion in how we view and live life. Making a decision that doesn't work could prompt you to try something else. You now have to move beyond the now, the *here*, and you have to go *there*.

It is scary to make changes, no doubt. Making one choice often means not being able to engage in a thousand other options. The grass always seems greener on the other side. Yet did you notice how rich and green your own grass is already? How large your field is?

Humans are living creatures with choices in life. We make simple, as well as complex and challenging, choices in life all of the time. Indecision steals our right to choose. Indecision prevents us from transitioning from the early phase 1 to the later phase 2 of adulthood. The old ways of thinking may stop you from reaching your fullest potential. Let's move from the first phase of adult life to the next. Decide now to change your procrastinating lifestyle.

4

Why Self-Regulation Fails: How You're Your Own Worst Enemy

Procrastination is the fear of success. People procrastinate because they are afraid of the success that they know will result if they move ahead now. Because success is heavy, carries a responsibility with it, it is much easier to procrastinate and live on the "someday I'll" philosophy.

—DENIS WAITLEY, MOTIVATIONAL SPEAKER

Waiting is a trap. There will always be reasons to wait. The truth is, there are only two things in life, reasons and results, and reasons simply don't count.

—DR. ROBERT ANTHONY

Procrastination: A Self-Sabotaging Technique?

According to a legend about the French Revolution, peasant workers in the factories jammed their wooden shoes into the gears of the machinery, in order to halt production. These shoes were called *sabots* in French, and the rebels were called "saboteurs." The act of damaging the property committed by these enemies of the nation was "sabotage." Today, psychologists use the term *self-sabotage* for situations where a person intentionally prevents his or her performance from resulting in a successful outcome.

Maybe you think your procrastination is helpful. It gets you going, motivates you to do future tasks; it even gives you a good "excuse" for not finishing tasks that are not quite perfect. You have a nice, believable, and plausible excuse to blame for any potential failure. The truth is, your procrastination is a self-sabotaging technique that psychologists label a *self-handicapping strategy*, and as a procrastinator, you engage in self-handicapping behaviors. Let's explore this concept.

Self-handicapping is a behavior pattern that was first studied systematically by social psychologists in the late 1970s and 1980s. These studies found that when people are given the opportunity, they actually place obstacles in their paths to inhibit the successful performance of a task (like those French rebels putting their wooden shoes into the cogs of the factory owner's machine). When people are unsure of whether they can maintain their successful performance in the future, they actively seek out and use obstacles that they can blame for poor performance.

Janet, a lawyer, has won a series of court cases, yet she is not confident that she can continue this successful streak. Consciously or subconsciously, Janet places obstacles in her path to impede future success: she chooses to play video games instead of writing and preparing an important future brief; she files motions late and fails to show up on time for a case. If she doesn't perform well in a trial, instead of her blaming her own insecurity and lack of self-confidence, she can blame the obstacle for her losing the case: the fact that she had little prep time, given her other tasks.

Janet chose an obstacle that she can use as an external, situational reason for her failure. In other words, this makes it possible for Janet and others to discount their inabilities or insecurities as a reason for their poor performance. Instead, they may assign blame to the obstacle.

Life is funny, though, and sometimes the expected failure does not occur. If Janet succeeds as a lawyer, despite the obstacles to her performance, she enhances her self-esteem (how Janet feels about herself). As I mentioned earlier, if others witness her success despite the obstacles, she can enhance her "social-esteem" (how others feel about her). In either case, Janet looks good—the self-handicap can function either to discount her own inabilities or to enhance her skills. ("I did it despite that obstacle.")

Do you think this story is too farfetched to be real? I read an August 2009 newspaper article about a Pennsylvania lawyer whose procrastination caused a local bar to lose its liquor license in July. The bar owner's new attorney summed it up well when he stated that his colleague had failed to file the required paperwork after several extensions, beginning in

April: "He was a procrastinator." Even if the bar reopens, the article stated, the liquor license cannot be granted, given state laws.

Can the cost of procrastinating fall on others? Yes—in this case, the bar owner couldn't operate his business. Does the procrastinator personally pay a price for his actions? Yes—there is now a public record of that attorney's procrastination, and current and future clients will be skeptical about trusting his abilities.

What does the procrastinating attorney have to say for himself? The article states that he claimed he had a family emergency just before he needed to file the July paperwork for the liquor license. That may be true, but you and I must ask, "Why didn't he file it in June? May? Or even back in April?" Had the attorney engaged in self-handicapping behavior?

So many times, people have told me that procrastination helps them and that they actually do well in life if they procrastinate. As I mentioned in an earlier chapter, there is a myth that if you wait until the last minute to buy airline tickets and book travel packages, they are cheaper than if purchased in advance. A *New York Times* story on September 9, 2009, indicated that the airlines have become wise to these procrastinating shoppers. Cheap near-term fares are getting harder to come by. Instead, airlines are running sales earlier and longer, and the numbers of last-minute plane seats are disappearing. Waiting does not pay off and can sabotage your plans.

Psychologists have used self-handicapping strategies to explain a variety of maladaptive behaviors. For instance, the alcoholic or the drug addict is likely to say, "It's not me, it's the booze or the drugs. If it wasn't for these substances, I could keep my job and be successful at work. I could be a good parent, have a happy family." Yet we don't know whether that is actually true, because the person with an addiction can use the booze or the drug as an excuse for his or her life failures. The individual has a ready-made handicap to attribute his or her failure to. These situations are prime examples of using handicaps, and they illustrate one type of self-handicapping strategy.

No Ifs, Ands, or Buts

At times, we all use wishful thinking to get through difficult life events. The British prime minister Harold McMillan was asked what undid his rule in the 1950s. His answer was, "Events, dear boy, events." Many people blame their shortcomings and failures on "the situation"—it's not my fault.

If only this were true. As I will discuss in chapter 7, people experience regret for not having accomplished things in life. They also report regret over having made poor decisions or having engaged in unwise acts. If only—so, they figure it's better to procrastinate.

X and Y were in the way. Many people proclaim reasons for why they procrastinate, why they failed to accomplish their tasks. They self-handicap and claim that certain obstacles prevented them from achieving their goals. "It's not my fault that I procrastinated. I could have done it, *but . . .*" People claim obstacles got in their way; they blame outside events, rather than themselves, for their procrastination. Moreover, they may think they are better and more accomplished than they actually are.

Are these valid reasons for why we procrastinate, or are they excuses we use to enable us to procrastinate? Perhaps, as Dr. Piers Steel from the University of Calgary proposed in chapter 1, when defining procrastination, excuses are "irrational reasons" that people give themselves and others for why they procrastinate.

Let's look into these various aspects of self-handicapping. Does "running late" count as "exercise"? It seems that busy people are the ones who show up on time for events. They know the value of time and realize that they cannot waste it. They are competent, and they get a lot done. For busy people, it's more than effective time management or being good at multitasking. Busy people don't make excuses whenever they fail to meet deadlines, because it is a rare occurrence for them.

Social psychologists, such as the late Dr. Charles R. (C.R.) Snyder from the University of Kansas, noted that some people claim handicaps. This is the basis of excuse making, something all of us have experienced. People attribute their failures not to themselves but to some character flaw they possess. For example, "I'm not a bad student, I'm just test anxious. I really could get A's and B+'s, but I just freeze during exams and get too anxious." Or, "People would like me more if I were less shy. It's just too hard for me to make friends." Dr. Snyder would say that these are excuses—self-handicaps that people claim they possess.

The cover of Dr. Snyder's popular book on excuse making, *Excuses: Masquerades in Search of Grace,* has always impressed me (see Snyder, Higgins, and Stuck 1983). It shows Adam and Eve holding the apple. What does that have to do with excuse making? Think about it: Adam and Eve were the first humans to make an excuse. They said that they disobeyed God's will not because they wanted to do things their way in Eden, but because a devil in the form of a snake made them eat the apple. "The devil made me do it," as the 1970s comedian Flip Wilson used to say. That's excuse making: "It's just not my fault; I can blame something or someone else for my failure."

What does all of this have to do with procrastination? It is amazing how many people blame their refusal to change their lives on external circumstances:

- I would get another job, but I need the familiarity, security, and the money from this one.
- I would be a more effective employee, but my boss stifles my creativity and new initiatives.
- I would improve my potential, but no one is willing to mentor me.
- I would improve my ability to interact with people, but I can't find the time.

What Motivates Self-Handicapping Behavior?

The relationship between procrastination and self-handicapping has a logical connection, and in a series of my early studies, I examined that relationship (Ferrari 1991a, 1991d, 1991e). The relationship makes sense because delaying the completion of a task often results in failure. The people I observed had used the delay as a convenient excuse: "I couldn't do well because I didn't have enough time." If people perform poorly on a task, they can blame it on not having enough time (thereby protecting their self-esteem by discounting the fact that they procrastinated). Yet in contrast, if the person performs well on the task despite the limited time, he or she will appear even more accomplished (thus enhancing the individual's self-esteem and social esteem among others who have witnessed the exceptional performance).

A significant relationship exists between procrastination and self-handicapping tendencies (Ferrari 1991a, 1992a). In an experiment with college-age women, I explored the use of self-handicapping behavior by procrastinators (Ferrari 1991d). Initially, all of the women worked on unsolvable but realistic-looking algebra and language art problems. Half of the women were told, "You did so well, compared to other students we've tested," while the other half received no feedback. The women were then told that they would work with or without loud, distracting noise on a second task. This second task was described as either highly revealing of their thinking ability or not revealing of ability at all. Finally, they were told that their performance on the task would be treated confidentially so that only they would know their skill level, or, conversely, that their performance would be scored by the researcher and the results made public.

Procrastinators, when compared to nonprocrastinators, were much more likely to choose the handicap of listening to distracting noise while working on the task. It's important to note that no one actually listened to the noise—once they made the choice, the study was over. All participants believed beforehand that if they chose to do so, they would be listening to noise while working on the task. Procrastinators compared to nonprocrastinators, however, were more likely to choose to listen to the "noise."

Thus, procrastinators (both men and women) chose obstacles to their performance when they were unsure of how they would perform on the second task—the procrastinators chose to self-handicap (Ferrari 1991e). And their reasons for delaying were really just excuses. It's essential to stop wasting energy on making excuses. Instead, use that energy to start and/or finish the task. Focus on what you can do to be more effective in your life.

You may use procrastination as a self-handicapping technique in ways you have not considered. For example, do you listen to music instead of studying without distractions? Then, if you fail, you can blame your poor test performance on the music. It makes sense, it's logical, and others will believe you. If, however, you succeed, you can really feel wonderful, knowing that you overcame the added burden of the distracting music while reading and studying for your exam.

Although you tell yourself that the music helps you focus, research for the last fifty years has shown that under these conditions, people's attention is divided and they are not able to focus as effectively as they think. Keep this in mind, and, instead, next time focus on the assignment. Remove all distractions. Consider this possible outcome: if you succeed and there were no distractions, imagine how proud you will feel. You did it on your own. And that feeling of pride is priceless.

Not surprisingly, procrastinators sabotage their performance more often than nonprocrastinators do. Yet procrastination itself is a handicap. Dr. Diane Tice, of Florida State University in Tallahassee, and I asked whether people used procrastination (delaying the start and/or completion of a task) as a self-handicapping strategy (Ferrari and Tice 2000). The short answer is yes. When women and men are given a chance to delay the start of a major task by playing video games or doing other enjoyable activities instead of beginning the task, both genders chose to delay starting the task—they self-handicapped their performance. Rather than work to prepare for a task described as difficult, these women and men procrastinated by engaging in a fun activity.

This study tells us that we sabotage what we have to do by procrastinating. Waiting is usually not winning. By procrastinating, you lose opportunities to achieve success in life. The act of procrastinating does not produce positive outcomes. And so, the next time you procrastinate on a task or some project that needs to be completed, ask yourself whether you are waiting to start or finish in order to have a nice believable "excuse" that others can point to, instead of blaming you, for the resulting failure.

To summarize, procrastinators self-handicap, and procrastination itself is a self-handicap. You don't increase the likelihood of doing well through this behavior; you merely have a convenient excuse in case you fail at the task down the road. Stop believing that your self-worth and your identity as a person depend solely on how well you perform tasks. There is no need to self-sabotage your skills, either in public or in private. Focus on what you can do, and improve your skills to achieve what you want to do. Build on the positive skills you already have that may contribute to success. Don't try to protect yourself from failure. Life is full of failure. Instead, ask yourself whether you can use the strengths you already possess to build on the likelihood of winning—of getting the job done.

Do You Fail to Self-Regulate?

Self-regulation is a term psychologists use to refer to someone's ability to keep his or her emotions, behaviors, and thoughts in check. For example, certain researchers focus on "mood regulation," or how people stay even-tempered: not too happy, not too sad. Self-regulation is the behavior we used to call "self-control." But the term *self-control* was considered too restrictive, so *self-regulation*—which has a broader meaning— was adopted. Chronic procrastination often results from our failure to self-regulate how we behave.

Procrastinators are unable to balance their ability to work effectively on a task and complete that task in a timely manner. Procrastinators are unable to delay their need for pleasure and to stay focused on the task at hand, as I showed in a couple of studies (Ferrari 2000, 2001; Ferrari and Pychyl 2007) and as supported by other procrastination researchers such as Dr. Timothy Pychyl of Carleton University. You might want to visit Dr. Pychyl's Web site at www.procrastination.ca for his podcasts on self-regulation and procrastination.

Buddhists call this being *mindful*. They suggest that we stay in the present and deal with life now. Are you worried about what to prepare for tomorrow night's dinner? It's okay to think about tomorrow, but not if you have only just finished today's dinner, the dirty dishes are still on the table, and the pots in the sink need to be scrubbed. Focus on the present, and enjoy the now. The dinner you finished was delicious. Your family and guests raved about how they liked it, and from the empty plates, you can see that they weren't lying. So, enjoy the moment.

Dr. Robert Emmons (UC Davis) and I conducted a survey study and a survey that explored the relationship between procrastination and not being able to practice self-control (Ferrari and Emmons 1995). We found that procrastination is directly related to low self-control and even low self-reinforcement. Self-reinforcement is your tendency to reward yourself for success (do you ever indulge in a sweet treat after completing a big project?). Interestingly, procrastinators claim that they cannot control their desires, and they tend not to reward themselves for the good things that happen to them.

Jamal loves to draw. Her major in school was studio art, and she has paintings and sculptures all over her apartment and her parents' home. Even when she needs to get to work by 9 a.m., she can be found walking in late because she spent the morning finishing her latest painting. Now, having such a wonderful interest is fine, but if Jamal can't delay the act of drawing to meet her employment responsibilities, that is a problem.

Moreover, when Jamal recently sold a piece of art that she had created, she told her best friend that it was nice, but she could not experience a deep feeling of satisfaction. Why? It seems Jamal could not reward herself for doing a good job. She did not experience self-reinforcement for finally selling a piece of her artwork.

Popular theories would have us believe that procrastinators are unable to engage in strong self-control or to delay their gratification. In other words, they experience a failure to self-regulate. Greg is seemingly unable to delay whatever he loves to do. He always wants to engage in fun activities before he works on frustrating chores. Although this technique may work on occasion, research has shown that it's usually better to get the more difficult things done first and then indulge in the pleasurable ones. Greg needs to put off playing the guitar or spending hours online with his friends in a group video game, until he first cleans his apartment, washes the car, or drops off his laundry at the dry cleaner.

The late great entrepreneur and philanthropist Dale Carnegie claimed that a key to his success was an ability to do the difficult tasks before the easy ones. The fun activities will be there later—but so will the hard, frustrating ones if you don't finish them first. If you do the difficult tasks first, you won't have to worry and ruminate about them while you're engaged in the fun ones. Consider the fun tasks your reward for finishing the difficult ones.

Procrastinators, compared to nonprocrastinators, don't have the ability to effectively regulate their performance and speed when they're restricted to working within a limited time frame (Ferrari 2001). Suppose you are asked to perform as best you can (increase your accuracy) while working as fast as possible (increase your speed) when there is a limited amount of time to perform the task: if you are a procrastinator, how will you perform? It seems that procrastinators are unable to maintain fast speed and be accurate. Instead, they perform poorly, making lots of errors and finishing few tasks. As I discussed earlier, the whole idea of working well under pressure is a myth.

You may hold the common belief that you "work best under pressure." You may feel that you can succeed at a task when you're given a limited amount of time to complete it—but you can't (see chapter 2, where this point is discussed). Limited time merely provides limited opportunities for you to find all of the resources you need.

Al is a news reporter who always seems to write his column close to its deadline. Whenever a story is due to be handed in to the editor on Friday morning, he starts collecting facts and conducting interviews on Wednesday afternoon and writes well into Thursday evening, possibly even very early on Friday morning. Al tells others that he writes best this way, because the increased arousal gets him moving and makes him productive. In truth, his stories are only acceptable. They could be better. He really could do more interesting investigative reporting and get a scoop on key interviews if he started earlier—even by a day—to give him more time to produce a better product.

When Al gets the assignment, he should sit down and make a list of what he needs to write the story. First, he could create an outline and then begin to fill in the holes, adding more and more details. Once he has an idea of what the story needs for completion, he can go from there. He doesn't have to devote all of his time to writing the story that first day. Instead, he can spend maybe 20 percent of the total time doing whatever is needed (e.g., research or writing the outline) and then add to that. The point is to start early and reduce the stress that would result from last-minute hyperactivity.

Here's one more example pertaining to the inability of decisional procrastinators—indecisives—to self-regulate their task
performance. Dr. Tim Pychyl of Carleton University and I compared decisional procrastinators and nonprocrastinators under
various experimental conditions (Ferrari and Pychyl 2007). As
I mentioned earlier in the chapter, decisional procrastinators,
compared to nonprocrastinators, weren't able to maintain a
successful balance in their speed and accuracy. In fact, over
time the indecisives became fatigued from making multiple
decisions, which negatively affected their ability to perform
future tasks. The notion of failure to self-regulate extends to
both behavioral and cognitive forms of procrastination. In
other words, when procrastinators try to control their speed
and accuracy under time constraints, they perform poorly and
begin to think negatively about themselves and their abilities.
In this book, I have asked you to build on your strengths and
your skills. If you apply this advice to your indecisiveness, this
means you should begin by making decisions that are easy and
simple, then gradually move to more complex decisions.

Even though these studies suggest that, at present, you may
be unable to balance, or regulate, your speed and accuracy
when working on a task, you can learn to improve these skills.
Set goals that are reachable for the tasks you have to do. Make
the goals concrete, and view them as attractive, as something
you want to do and to achieve—not as something to avoid.

Nothing happens overnight. If you view self-regulation
as a muscle that needs to be strengthened (as many current
researchers in this field propose), then you will realize that
you need to exercise the muscle. You must focus on building
your strengths in order to get things done. Exercising your self-
regulation muscle strengthens your willpower.

As I've said many times, procrastination is learned, so it
can be unlearned. In addition, you can do several things at

once—it's called multitasking. Multitasking is a skill and an art that you can learn. On the Ed Sullivan TV show in the 1960s, Ed introduced many acts each Sunday night. When I was a child, I remember seeing a man juggle bowling pins while spinning a dozen dishes in the air and rotating a chair on the tip of his nose—an early form of multitasking. No one asks that you spin dishes or balance chairs on your face, but you can learn to work on two tasks at a time. Start with something as simple as listening to music while you work, or working at your laptop while you answer questions from people around you. Be careful, though, to use good judgment about when multitasking is a more efficient use of your time or when doing two things at once is too distracting. If you are studying for an exam, you need to focus all of your attention on that task. Talking to others, texting, or playing music will divert your mind and hinder your full concentration.

I'm sure you've heard of the famous Chinese proverb "Don't bite off more than you can chew." There was wisdom in this expression, because many Chinese peasants were so poor and so hungry that they took large bites of food whenever it was available. But then the people could not chew or swallow, and breathing was difficult because their mouths were overstuffed. Over time, however, Western cultures changed the meaning of that proverb to imply that one should never overextend oneself. Now the proverb seems to warn that if you set limits that are too high, too demanding, and too difficult to reach, you simply can't achieve your goal. Consequently, you will fail. And if you fail often, you will then give up and stop trying.

Yet the situation is usually more complicated than that. Sometimes you need to both reach for the stars with your big dreams and also take a step-by-step, one-day-at-a-time approach. If you tell yourself your dreams are impossible, it becomes a self-fulfilling prophecy, predicting your defeat. So keep the dream alive, in your macrocosmic bird's-eye perspective, but put your daily focus on achievable goals that will bring you closer to the main objective.

No one is perfect—and no one has to be. But we need to be able to handle the complexities around us, when several things are often happening at once. Poor self-regulation accompanies many personal problems besides procrastination, such as addiction to drugs, tobacco, caffeine, food, gambling, and more. Learning to self-regulate will help you eliminate procrastination from your life.

Perfection Is Pure Fiction

Nothing is so fatiguing as the eternal
hanging on of an uncompleted task.

—WILLIAM JAMES

He who hesitates is—last.

—MAE WEST

Postpone: Not a good action.

—IRISH PROVERB

Leonardo da Vinci carried the *Mona Lisa* around with him for twenty years before he finished putting on the final brush strokes. Michelangelo's perfectionism gave us masterpieces that have been enjoyed for centuries. Were these artists so busy they could not finish their work? Or were they *perfectionists*, afraid to add the last stroke, the last touch on a sculpture? To finish their piece of art would mean that it now would be exposed for the world to see. What if others did not like or appreciate the artwork—could the artists handle the public rejection? Historians suggest that da Vinci and Michelangelo were perfectionists.

On the one hand, perfectionism can drive you to achieve exceptional things, even in the face of obstacles. On the other hand, it can be a huge productivity killer.

For a number of years, three of my research colleagues, from different perspectives, have examined perfectionism. Dr. Randy Frost, from Smith College in Massachusetts, looked at the consequences of perfectionism and the perceptions of perfectionists. Frost's research explored perfectionism as a cognitive perception about how to view a task. The team of Drs. Gordon Flett of York University in Toronto and Paul Hewitt of the University of British Columbia in Vancouver took a separate but related angle. They looked at the origins of perfectionism, whether it arose from standards imposed by others, society, or oneself.

As Dr. Flett has said recently, perfectionists try to maintain high standards in all that they do. But over time, keeping to high standards and then trying to improve on what is already "perfect" causes perfectionists to burn out—they simply can't maintain their perfectionism. As a result, the time increases between when they form an intention to act and then actually engaging in the behavior. Perfectionist procrastinators will delay finishing the task. In other words, trying to maintain a sense of perfectionism causes procrastinators to delay or not finish a task because they simply can't continue to be perfect. The combination of perfectionism and procrastination is deadly, since standards of excellence are imposed causing one to never finish. Sure, da Vinci and Michelanglo were outstanding artists who created masterpieces, but as we see they also never finished or delayed finishing pieces of work that the world at their time could not enjoy. We are fallible, we make mistakes. In turn, we must strive for being "partially perfect."

I don't know how Mary Poppins did it, because she was "practically perfect in every way." For the rest of us mere mortals, maintaining a life of perfection is impossible. Researchers have concluded from studies of perfectionism that it is a hindrance to one's having a good quality of life, because perfectionism is not obtainable or maintainable. Perfectionism is pure fiction. Mary Poppins is fictional; she never lived in New York, L.A., or Chicago. And she would not have made it today in modern London, either.

None of us is perfect, nor should we be. Our idiosyncrasies make us interesting individuals. You are you because of your strengths and weaknesses, the life experiences you have had, and your goals, values, and visions. There can never be another you because no one, not even a clone, has the same life experiences that you do. I am not suggesting that you seek mediocrity or strive to be average (although there is nothing wrong with being average). Instead, all of us should use the talents we possess to improve the lives of others.

Knowing the difference between what is important to get right and what is less important may save you lots of time and countless headaches. Getting your tax returns right, with the important information organized and the figures double-checked, is a wise thing to do. It's not important, however, to have a perfectly made bed or a totally organized kitchen pantry. If you stop aiming for perfectionism in trivial matters, you'll be amazed at the amount of extra time you will have. Instead, focus on the benefits of finishing the project. Break the project down into smaller parts, and accomplish each bite-size task. Once you start to make progress, you are much more likely to keep going until you finish.

Consider the notion of self-actualization that is espoused by humanistic psychology. This concept implies that we must be the best we can be and then enhance it—become even better. But wait, if you are already being the best you can be, achieving 100 percent of what you set out to do, how can you make yourself even better? It does not make sense. Instead, strive to be the best you can be. Realize that you will *never* be perfect, but nevertheless try to achieve this goal. Always remember, however, that it is okay *not* to be perfect. Perfectionism is pure fiction.

We will never reach the exalted state of being the best we can be, but we must try. As psychologists often say, strive to reach 80 percent of your goals. That's better than average and better than mediocrity. Yet it is not perfect. Try to take pride when you reach at least 80 percent of your goals. Next time, try again to do your best and as much as you can. When you fail, don't beat yourself up.

The measure of a person is not whether he or she wins, but how that individual handles failure. How well do you rise (like a phoenix) from the ashes of life's disappointments and disasters to pick yourself up and start again? If you can get your office organized or your car cleaned 80 percent of the way, that is enough. Your daily activities will clutter the office again, and the car will get dirty again (just ask any parent who has young children). Don't get uptight if the papers on the desk are not exactly in the right piles, or you have not detailed your car's interior or exterior to 100 percent standards of perfection. Ask yourself whether life would still go on with the desk and the car at 80 or maybe 85 percent cleanliness (if that is a better comfort level for you). You do not need to be perfect.

Let me be clear, because this relates to procrastination—you do not need to work on the same task over and over again (to be overly persistent). Instead, get the "chores of life" (like a clean desk and a clean car) in very good condition (that 80 percent rule again) and enjoy the satisfaction of a job well done. Some people don't even begin chores because they think they can never finish them or get them perfect. Again, achieving 80 percent of your goals is good enough. No one is perfect.

The Perfection-Procrastination Link

Some procrastinators say, "I am not a procrastinator, I am a perfectionist. Unless the task is done perfectly, I don't want to finish it or hand it in." Yes, there is a relationship between procrastination and perfectionism. The motivation for perfectionism differs greatly, however, depending on whether you are a procrastinator or a nonprocrastinator (Ferrari 1992a). Nonprocrastinators are motivated to produce the best possible product and strive for perfectionism for this reason.

For procrastinators, however, perfectionist tendencies are a result of trying to present themselves as hard-working individuals. To ingratiate themselves to others, procrastinators claim that they delay completing projects because they are motivated by perfectionism. In other words, both procrastinators and nonprocrastinators can be perfectionists (McCloskey, Pychyl, and Ferrari 2008). To say, then, that I am a perfectionist and that is why I procrastinate is pure fiction. As a procrastinator, it's important for you to take a hard look at your true motivations and determine whether you're being realistic.

The perfectionism of procrastinators is motivated by a desire to belong and be liked by others; they justify their procrastination by saying that delays will result in a better outcome. For nonprocrastinators, perfectionism is motivated by a desire "to get ahead," to produce the best possible product, regardless of what others may think. There is no strong need to please others and be known as a hard worker.

Heidi wants everyone to like her. She shops for days looking for the best birthday gifts for everyone she knows. And, in turn, she never manages to get those gifts for friends and family delivered on the date of the actual birthdays. Her drive toward perfectionism keeps her from completing tasks on time. Clark, instead, likes to buy his birthday gifts for family and friends from a good-quality store, where the items may cost more, but they last a long time. He meets his goal of being sure the post office has time to mail the gifts to arrive on or just before the birth date. Clark is a nonprocrastinator, but he seeks to be perfect by trying to find a durable gift that the recipient will really like.

You don't need to use perfectionism as an excuse for being a procrastinator. When you claim that you are a perfectionist and that's why you can't finish a task, what you're really telling the world is that you want to protect your social esteem—you need to have others feel good about you. By not completing the task (even though you may be showing others that you are now late and rushed at the last minute), you seem to be trying to make others like you by showing them that you are working hard.

When Heidi phones her friend once again to tell him that his birthday gift will be late, she makes sure to mention that its lateness is due to the amount of time she spent shopping for something he will really like. She wants her friends and family to like her for trying to buy the perfect gift. What Heidi fails to realize is that people like her because she is Heidi, with all of her character flaws and foibles. She is a good person, even if she is not perfect.

The Fallout from Coworkers (and the Boss) When Procrastinators Claim to Be Perfectionists

Does this image of perfectionism actually help procrastinators? Will others, for example, your coworkers, like you more if you try to be perfect?

I examined procrastination in the workplace (Ferrari 1992b). Men and women working in corporate settings throughout New York City completed a procrastination survey and evaluated a vignette featuring a character named Mr. Nolan. Mr. Nolan was a happily married man whose personal life was fine. Mr. Nolan never submitted reports or projects on time, however; he always delayed the beginning of important tasks. Whenever he was asked about those assignments, he would say, "I'm working on them."

Do you sound like Mr. Nolan at your job? Do you know other coworkers who resemble Mr. Nolan where you work? How do you respond to others' inquiries when they ask, "Are you done yet?" I ended the vignettes in this study by telling participants that Mr. Nolan gave himself one of three labels: procrastinator, perfectionist, or neither (no label). Participants then had to rate Mr. Nolan on whether he was responsible for his work-related failures, as well as on whether he should be allowed to continue in his corporate role or be fired.

I wanted to learn how procrastinators, compared to nonprocrastinators, would rate and evaluate other procrastinators at their place of employment who self-identified using the more socially accepted word *perfectionist* versus the term *procrastinator*. The outcome of this study has real-world implications. Suppose you are a procrastinator—but your boss is also a procrastinator. Every year when you have your annual merit raise review, will your boss go easier on your evaluation because he or she is just like you? Or will your boss be harder on you at the time of your evaluation? Does it matter whether you call yourself a perfectionist?

It did not matter what Mr. Nolan called himself. Both nonprocrastinators and procrastinators evaluated Mr. Nolan harshly. They suggested that he was the cause for company's failures, he was responsible for his acts and poor performance, and, most interestingly, they wanted him fired. It did not matter whether Mr. Nolan was labeled a procrastinator or a perfectionist. Folks wanted him gone. When you realize that even fellow procrastinators rated Mr. Nolan negatively, these results become more profound.

You won't receive sympathy from peer procrastinators by calling yourself a perfectionist. Don't expect an easier time if your boss is a procrastinator. Your boss will not cut you any slack. In fact, the procrastinating boss will be harder on procrastinators than on other employees.

Perhaps your boss does not embrace or excuse your procrastination because she wants to distance herself from other procrastinators. Maybe she is reflecting a sense of dislike for her own behavior. Whatever the reason, other procrastinators will not favor their peers who procrastinate. What it comes down to is that no one likes procrastinators—so why be one?

You can't blame perfectionism for your procrastination. Even some nonprocrastinators are perfectionists. If your perfectionism leads you to take on extra tasks because you think others will like you more, then don't bother, because they won't. Let others like you for all of your faults and your frailties. You're human.

You make mistakes; no one is perfect. It may be a cliché, but it's true. It's a myth, pure fiction, that anyone can be perfect. You are human, not superhuman. In addition, if you think by your claiming to be perfect, others will understand and excuse your procrastination, they won't. In fact, if they are procrastinators, too, and have some role in evaluating you, they will come down hard on you for procrastinating, even if you claim you're a perfectionist.

End the cycle of perfectionism-procrastination simply by remembering that you are *you*. Your identity is not based on your being perfect. Not everyone will like you, and that is okay.

Perfectionism causes you to miss deadlines, be too picky, have difficulty making decisions, avoid commitments, lose opportunities, feel dissatisfied with life, be guarded in relationships, and constantly worry and ruminate. You need to accept that life has time constraints, and it's reasonable to be "good enough," given the deadline and your other commitments.

Although you cannot be perfect, you *can* be a person who does the best you can, using the signature strengths you possess. See the positives. You're probably an expert at noticing the flaws in your own work and in everything around you. For everything you see that you don't like, find something that you appreciate and focus on that. Put things into perspective. Are the tasks you delay because of a need to be perfect really that important? Will anyone even remember them in ten minutes?

Remember that other people value us not only because of what we do for them and for ourselves. We are also valuable because of our strengths—and our weaknesses. Together, these qualities make us the interesting people that we are. We all will encounter failure in our lives, but we must nevertheless do what we can to improve the lives of others.

Does Technology Make It Easier to Procrastinate?

Even if you're on the right track—you'll get run
over if you just sit there.

—WILL ROGERS

———————

The way to get started is to quit talking
and begin doing.

—WALT DISNEY

Technology: The New Thief of Time

Perhaps you believe that technology has set you free. Maybe you think that our age of high-tech gadgets has made it virtually impossible to procrastinate, because we need to respond to more messages and do more tasks more often for more people.

In fact, the opposite is true. Basex, a company that explores the efficiency of workers at information-intensive companies (that is, high-tech, computer-based companies), produced a report featured in the *New York Times* in 2008. The report stated that 28 percent of the average day an office worker spent in the office was interrupted by some form of technology. Employees reported that these interruptions were unnecessary and not urgent.

Instead, people seem to be procrastinating at similar, if not higher, rates than in the past. Yet the comfort you feel from procrastinating will only keep you from reaching your full potential. If you procrastinate to feel good and to avoid experiencing anxiety from doing a task or feeling tired from working on something, then you are missing the joys and pleasures that result from doing a job well. You are focused on negative emotions like fear and missing out on positive emotions, such as pride and satisfaction.

Some people press that snooze button on the alarm clock to gain nine extra minutes of sleep. Occasionally pressing that button once or maybe even twice is fine. But if you find yourself pressing it over and over and over, before you know it two hours have gone by. That's not a good thing.

The TV remote was once an expensive option that was available on only a few television sets. Fifty years ago, you had to get out of your comfortable chair and walk across the room all the way to the TV set to change the channel—by hand! Today, most TVs cannot even be turned on and off unless you use the remote. The TV remote operates every part of the system. Life without a remote is an unbearable option for many people. Moreover, there are now remotes that operate just about all of the electronics in your home (TV, DVD, video player, stereos, lights, electrical systems, you name it). Try hiding the TV remote, and see what happens in your family. It can get pretty ugly pretty quickly.

There was a time when we had no choice but to use snail mail—to go to the local post office and mail our important documents. We had to plan on sending that document or letter two or three days before it was supposed to arrive. Now, we can e-mail the item as an attachment. We instant message a person with something that is so important that we think our lives depend on getting it there within seconds. Does this sound like you?

Do you have a Facebook or a MySpace account? How often do you check for new "friends" who visit and write? The age of privacy has been lost, as we spend more and more time checking out whether others are contacting us. Our "real-time" friendships may get lost in a virtual world.

Consider the cable network news stations. Today they report the news on the main screen, with a band along the bottom giving us additional news, plus a box inside the screen with more information. We are being fed more and more information through technology. We want it now; we want it when we want it. We don't want to wait. We want comfort, and we want it instantly.

But instead of gaining time as a result of technology, we're losing it. A 2008 article in the *Chicago Tribune* indicated that 46 percent—nearly half—of today's workers claimed that cell phones, e-mail, and the Internet have led to an increased demand on their time. As a result, we end up working more—longer hours and more days. Like perfectionism, our sense of being liberated by technology is an illusion—at least, when it comes to procrastination. Earlier, I noted that no one is perfect and no one will ever achieve perfection (see chapter 5). Similarly, you cannot expect technology to solve all of the planet's problems to create a perfect world.

This raises the question, which you need to consider: has technology really made you less of a procrastinator? Have Facebook, texting, Twitter, or instant messaging made you more productive? Although one could argue that these examples of technology have made our lives more comfortable and easier, procrastination continues to exist.

At least a couple of recent research studies have established a link between procrastination and Internet use. One study found that online browsing as procrastination—which the authors call "e-procrastination"—is related to attitudes like a sense of low control over one's time and a desire to take risks by visiting Web sites that are forbidden. Such e-procrastination leads to impulsivity in purchasing things online that are not needed (Negra, Mzoughi, and Bouhlel 2008). The use of the Internet can interrupt one's tasks and flow of thoughts, resulting in problematic outcomes (Wretschko and Fridjhon 2008).

Did you know there is even a technology that will help you procrastinate? My daughter, who noticed me writing this section of the book, just told me that Mac laptops contain an application called "iProcrastinate," so that Mac users can link to ways to procrastinate. For only three dollars, you can get an iPhone application called "Put Things Off." It lets you delay things for a fixed time, anywhere from 1 to 31 days. So now we as a culture have a new way to embrace procrastination.

Technology Can Prevent or Promote Procrastination

It should be noted that in some cases, technology may actually help people *stop* procrastinating. For instance, a manufacturer recently created an alarm clock that reminds folks when to wake up. Called the "Neverlate Alarm Clock," it fits every schedule by providing wake-up alerts at different times for every day of the week. Imagine, if you're a college student you'll never be late for class—just set the clock for your weekly morning classes, and you will be awakened on a variable schedule. The clock also has a nap timer, if you want to take a few winks between classes.

Another example of helpful technology is a computer program called "Instant Boss" that you can download for free. This application may help you stay on task, because you set a running timer to manage your work and break periods. The program can be set for as long as you want before taking a break (say, for fifteen or twenty minutes), then you can set the timer for the length of time the break period should last (maybe five minutes) and how many times you want to repeat this cycle (e.g., four times in a two-hour period).

You have to return to the task when the break is over, though. But if you have attention difficulties or are easily distracted, you might never get back on task. That short break becomes a permanent vacation. Remember, the purpose of a break is to recharge your battery, to reinvigorate your work. Use the free time wisely, and then get back to the task at hand.

I buy an annual weekly appointment book called a "Day Minder," printed by the Mead Company. I don't use an electronic planner to keep a record of what I have to do. I like to write my plans in my appointment book. Call me old-fashioned, but it works for me. Inside the planner on the first page is a neat advertising statement that I think sums up the topic of technology and time. The Mead Company states that its goal is to help you manage "today's most precious commodity—your time. Although we can't put more hours in the day or days in the week, we . . . develop products that keep you organized and make you more productive."

You still can use technology to help you be more effective. Don't get me wrong; technology can help you reach your unrealized potential. Technology can be a useful tool and can make you more effective—if you use it correctly. For instance, at work you can limit the amount of time you spend checking e-mail. I heard of one company where employees are allowed to check e-mail only during the last ten minutes of each hour, instead of every ten minutes. Another company recommends that all employees check e-mail messages only once every ninety minutes. Follow one of these three actions for every e-mail message you read: read and delete, read and reply, or read and file for later work. You should empty your e-mail inbox after every time you check it. Keep a clean e-mail inbox. If there are no new messages when you check, great; use the time to take a quick break for coffee or something to eat. Maybe you could even get around to that other task you've been putting off.

I walked into a colleague's office a month ago, and I noticed that he had two monitors connected to his desktop computer. I asked him why he needed all of that screen space. He said that this enabled him to keep a number of applications open at once and it saved him time. Dual monitors allow you to work in two full windows concurrently. I've heard that people's effectiveness goes up as much as 50 percent when they can view e-mail and their client account screen at the same time. In a case like this, technology helps us be more productive.

Getting Organized: Your Secret Weapon in Task Completion

As you have seen, technology does not necessarily help you accomplish tasks. Often, technology is a major distraction.

There are simple, old-fashioned methods you can use to get organized and be more efficient. As I will explain in detail in chapter 7, you really can't manage time—you have to manage yourself. You can and must control the elements in your environment that cause you to procrastinate.

So, what can you do to be more organized? You need to discover what works best for you, but I found a number of Web sites and links that offer suggestions on becoming more organized and on procrastinating less. Here are a few suggestions:

- *Create a sense of time urgency for the tasks you need to get done.* Give yourself a reason to stop procrastinating. Perhaps you want to impress your family and friends, or maybe you will be in a better situation financially if you pay off your bills early. Or you might experience less stress and worry if you arrive on time for work and appointments.
- *Figure out how long the task will take.* Perhaps you put off working on a task because you're afraid of how long it

will take to complete it. Review similar projects you did in the past and gauge how long it took you to finish those tasks successfully. For instance, if it required five hours of studying for the good grade you earned the last time, then consider that it will take five hours again to study for this new class.

- *Jot down a to-do list.* Then make the list smaller with a "To Do Today" list for the present day. This idea *might* work; I'm not a big fan of its use because some procrastinators generate multiple lists, over and over again. I have the same feeling about a planner. But if you can restrict yourself to just one list, and you keep the number of tasks realistic and attainable (e.g., five things usually work well) or use your planner regularly and then prioritize the items on the list, based on what you need to accomplish sooner, rather than later, it might work. Maybe you can work backward from the due date or the deadline. Break the task down into parts to set a weekly or daily backward countdown of specific (observable and behavioral) acts that need to be completed by each step. This way, you know exactly where you stand every day and week.

- *Hold yourself accountable for getting things done.* If you don't accomplish at least 80 percent of your goals, then you will not reward yourself with a fun activity that you want to do. A coach or a mentor might help motivate you, but the bottom line is that *you* are responsible for your behavior. As Gandhi said, "Seek the change you want to see."

- *Keep your desk and workplace decluttered.* Leave nothing on your desk except what you are working on now. Keep only the materials you need for the current project within reach. Place all other materials in a file cabinet or a box for storage.

- *Throw away the trash.* Get rid of things you don't need.
- *Recognize the times in your work plan when you must focus on other tasks and your routine will be disrupted.* Don't seek to be perfect (reread chapter 5). Obstacles are always present. But knowing what distracts you makes it easier for you to find alternative routes to success.
- *For truly unpleasant tasks, give yourself fifteen-minute blocks of time to accomplish them.* In just fifteen minutes each morning and evening, you can review, sort, do certain tasks quickly, and assign longer times to accomplish others.
- *Prioritize.* Not everything has to be done immediately, but do the things you need to do. And do them in order, if that is necessary. Do A tasks before B tasks, and do B tasks before C tasks. Never tackle something unimportant first merely because you can get it done quickly.
- *Don't be a "people pleaser" and feel that you must say yes to every request that you receive at work or at home.* It's okay to say no. Delegate if you must.
- *Reward yourself if you accomplish 80 percent or more of your to-do list.* Have lunch with an old friend, take in a movie, eat a hot-fudge sundae, buy tickets for a concert. Just remember, tomorrow you will have more tasks to accomplish. Life is like that.

There are even new technologies that may help you not procrastinate. It isn't the use of technology but its *misuse* that is the problem. Don't use technology as an excuse for procrastination. Don't blame the machine. Instead, let technology help you accomplish your goals in life.

Your alarm clock's snooze button is not to blame for your oversleeping. You simply have to limit how often you press the button. Here is a simple suggestion that experts have recommended for decades. Put the alarm clock at the other end of the room so that you need to actually get up to shut it off. You will not be able to press the snooze button over and over to extend your time in bed from nine extra minutes (the usual length of time for a snooze alarm) to twenty-nine minutes. And don't use music as your wake-up call. The soft jazz you hear might keep you in bed. Instead, use that annoying buzzer so that you have to cross the room to turn it off. This is no guarantee that you won't simply flop back into bed, but once you are up, you are more likely to stay up. You'll procrastinate less and spend less time in bed if you have to exert energy to get things done in the morning.

Here is another situation in which technology can prevent you from procrastinating. If you have ever been a speaker on a panel (say, you're the fourth speaker out of four participants), you know that some people run longer than others. Every speaker is given fifteen minutes to cover all of his or her points and to answer a couple of questions after the presentation. If you are the last one to speak, you know that you often have much less than fifteen minutes' time. So you panic and find yourself rushing through the slides you've prepared and the points you wanted to make.

Consider a new "clicker," which speakers can use to advance their PowerPoint slide presentations. At a recent conference I participated in, each of us on the panel was handed a remote control clicker that not only included forward and backward advance buttons but also had a timing system. Speakers felt a vibration (similar to when a cell phone silently vibrates to let you know you have a call) to tell them to move forward. The remote could also be set to let the speaker know that he or she had only two or five minutes left for the presentation.

Now, with this new clicker, the speakers would be cued to stop or move on or wrap up the presentation soon. I don't know whether the following option was included in the remote controls, but I suggest adding a feature to make the screen go blank when the time limit is reached (of fifteen minutes, in the case of this particular presentation), so that speakers realize they *must* end immediately. (By the way, I never felt the buzzer go off because I finished my presentation with sixty seconds to spare.)

Facebook, e-mail, Twitter, and instant messaging can distract us from tasks we need to accomplish. Yet there is another new software program that limits the amount of time you can spend checking e-mail or on the Internet when you are supposed to be working on word-processing programs. You can configure that software so that you can receive messages only from the boss or your spouse, in case of emergencies. All other people who contact you or want your attention—such as a friend who wants to show you the latest sport scores or invite you to a Web game—get filtered out.

Dr. Piers Steel, from the University of Calgary, says that certain triggers make us procrastinate. In psychology, those triggers or cues have been called "stimuli" ("discriminative stimuli," if we want to be technical). Psychologists use the term *stimulus control* when referring to the act of changing something in the patient's environment that prevents a behavior from occurring. That stimulus was a "trigger" that prompted the act to happen. I believe you can learn to control the stimuli that precede your actions. If you can prevent the behavior from happening, then other actions (ideally, those you want to happen) are more likely to take place.

As I've said many times, you *can* change. You can control those triggers or cues (those stimuli) that make you procrastinate. Identify the triggers, recognize when they occur, and change them. You have the power to make your life better. Technology can help you stop procrastinating. Use it to set up your environment so that you don't procrastinate.

Be Faster, but Not Frantic

Over the years, I've noticed that people (or maybe only younger people?) always seem to be looking for the fastest technology—whatever can perform tasks more quickly. The computer with a CPU that processes three seconds faster is better than the model that came out last year. The printer that produces one page more a minute is more desirable than the model from six months ago that makes us wait three seconds longer for that extra page. Think of the fax machine—do many people even use them today?

Yet the question needs to be asked—is faster better? Samantha Ettus, in her 2009 book *The Experts' Guide to Doing Things Faster*, notes that faster does not mean people are getting more from life. She says that the point is not to rush or be frantic, not to have your head spinning as you try to accomplish too much. Faster means being more strategic with your time, and that includes being more efficient.

If we relate this notion of speed to procrastination, it means that you can be more efficient and effective in what you do. Everyone wants a better life and a way to get more from life. But rushing is not the answer. Instead, I ask that procrastinators change the way they think—open themselves up to new ideas, drop ineffective ways of doing things, end their habit of delaying, and get on with living their lives.

Consider these simple suggestions that Ettus offers to improve the quality of your life, if you only have ten minutes:

- Do some exercise.
- Open a bottle of wine with ease.
- Make a brownie.
- Chop vegetables safely.
- Take the kids out to eat.

- Teach your dog a new trick.
- Get fast-but-fresh food.
- Clean your microwave.
- Pay three bills.

Kathy Lockett offers Executive Style Management on her Web site and asks her clients at work to "Make friends with your diary." Every day, schedule the first hour of the day as an appointment with yourself. Learn to treasure that hour as your special time. Don't fill it with e-mail, paperwork, or appointments with clients, coworkers, or the boss. Use this hour realistically; use it for yourself.

Now, break that first work hour into six ten-minute, quick-and-dirty chunks of time:

- *At work:* Return phone calls; clear your desk by filing papers, photocopying an important document, drafting a letter, or finding information for a colleague.
- *At home:* Toss out all expired food in the pantry; clean out two refrigerator shelves, organize a junk drawer, set up a recipe mini-filing system for the kitchen, restack the tools in the garage.

You will surprise yourself with what you can do in those six blocks of time. Don't multitask. Instead, focus on one task at a time and get it finished before you start on the next one.

After a few days of these hour-long self-appointments, Lockett claims that you will be in a groove to get the little-but-important daily stuff done and will feel much less stress and anxiety about your workload. If you can use these ten-minute slots to get one task done per session without worrying about the next job or straying into reading unnecessary e-mail, you'll find that your first hour will be very productive.

If you must, put the task of opening, reading, and responding to e-mail last on your list of things to do. Actually, make it number 7 on your list, after the six ten-minute sessions.

Using Technology Wisely

Technology has been around for decades and has the potential to make us more effective. Being human, however, we tend to use technology as a nice ready-made excuse for delaying ("It's not my fault. The printer 'died' last night, so I couldn't get the report done today."). In fact, some technologies now exist to help us procrastinate.

We can't add more time to our lives. Yet we can use the time we have wisely. In the next chapter, I will discuss our perception of time and how procrastinators try to choose tasks that work to their advantage.

Some interesting T's that can get you in trouble if not monitored are technology, time, and tasks, especially if you are a procrastinator. Remember, instead, this handy T—*technology is a tool*. Technology can help you live your life and, in most cases, pursue happiness more effectively. It can help you reach your goals. It is a means to an end. We get in trouble when we make various advances in technology the end goal, and we lose sight of our humanness. So, don't procrastinate by using technology—let technology help you be more efficient.

Why the Time of Day and the Tasks That Need to Be Done Matter to Procrastinators

What may be done at any time will be done
at no time.

—SCOTTISH PROVERB

———————

You don't have to see the whole staircase,
just take the first step.

— MARTIN LUTHER KING JR.

———————

Tomorrow is often the busiest day of the week.

—SPANISH PROVERB

L et's be honest—can you really "manage your time"? There are so many self-help books that try to teach us to be more productive and efficient. I am not against those important life goals, but the idea of managing time is another fiction, like the pursuit of perfection. Sure, you can invest in a BlackBerry or a planner and keep track of your daily activities—but will that give you *more* time?

Human beings perceive time as being constant. There are 168 hours in a week. We've always had 24 hours in a day, and for centuries, we've talked about 7 days a week (well, except for the Beatles, who sang a song in the late 1960s called "Eight Days a Week"). You might find it interesting to know that our current calendar of days and months has been the same for the past 428 consecutive years, based on the Gregorian calendar. Pope Gregory XIII promoted the calendar we use, something he modified from Julius Caesar's calendar, in 1582, as something better than what was used during his time. Still, this calendar is not perfect, because every four years (except centuries not divisible by 400) we need to add an extra day to accommodate for Gregory's leap-year formula. But let's not take any more time to digress.

Some procrastinators say, "I just don't have the time." My response is, "Yes, you have time. You have the same amount of time as nonprocrastinators. We all have the same amount of time each week. If you sleep for eight hours a night and work forty hours a week (boy, are you lucky if you can spend eight hours asleep and only forty at work!), that leaves seventy-two hours a week for other tasks."

We can't stop or control time, even though so many science-fiction movies and stories try to show us that time travel is possible. Time is like a stream, constantly flowing. As you read this paragraph, seconds have passed, and the present instantly becomes the past.

If we can't manage time, can we at least learn to become more efficient with the time we have? How do we handle waiting for things in life to happen? You see, it is not time but rather ourselves that we need to manage more effectively.

Professor Fuschia M. Sirois, PhD, from Bishop's University in Quebec, is a respected research psychologist who explores procrastination and its impact on health behaviors. More recently, Dr. Sirois conducted studies on how folks "blame it on time" when they can't get something done (Sirois 2007). You have undoubtedly heard people say that lack of time prevented them from doing something. Does that sound like an excuse that you, as a procrastinator, tell yourself?

I agree with Dr. Sirois: procrastinators have lots of time. They have the same amount of time as everyone else. Yet procrastinators often blame their delays and their inability to complete their tasks on not having enough time.

Journalist Laura Vanderkam, in her new book *168 Hours*, offers some good suggestions on using one's time. For instance, she suggests viewing time broadly. Often at work, we see that something is due on Friday, but we don't consider the project to have components that may be completed on Tuesday, Wednesday, and Thursday. It makes sense to use the whole week to complete the task. Vanderkam also claims we don't use our leisure time well. If there are breaks between tasks or assignments, we should take that break and "chill." We should focus on the free time we have at that moment, so that when we return to our target task, we won't feel guilty or get upset about working on it.

As I gathered information and material to write this book, I read some marvelous suggestions on how to deal with one of the largest time suckers that exists in business settings: *meetings*. We probably spend twice as much time in meetings as we need to. We love meetings. We even have meetings to decide when to have a meeting. And it seems as though everyone at the meeting has something to say. At least, people *think* they have something to say. For instance, someone makes a point that we either agree or disagree with, and then everyone needs to say something about the new idea. The more people there are at the meeting, the more we go around and around with the same comments. How many times have you heard someone say, "I agree with that idea/point." And then the person restates the same point in different words. Don't let this happen at your next meeting.

Take charge of the meeting. I think that people who are chronically late to meetings need a little shaming and should pay actual fines. If someone is late, consider appointing him or her the leader for a boring organizational assignment (such as evaluating the company logo and letterhead on stationery), and paying a small penalty (the late person needs to arrive five minutes early the next time, with coffee for everyone).

Meetings are for conversations and discussions. E-mails are to provide information. Start the meeting on time. And if someone comes in late, fine the person $10. End on time. If the ninety-minute meeting runs longer, get up and walk out. One blog suggested that a meeting be held where there are no chairs and everyone must stand. Folks will get tired very quickly, and the meeting will end early.

In essence, when a meeting runs over the time limit, a trust has been broken. There was a general agreement to meet during this time block and someone broke their commitment to stick to that time frame. To stay on course, require people to submit a prioritized agenda with a time allotment for each item.

Time is an asset, and we cannot buy more of it. Invest time. Don't spend it (see my Ferrari 2010 book chapter on time management for other ideas on time).

The Value of Waiting

For many children, waiting for Santa Claus to arrive on Christmas morning is a tough experience. For some adults, waiting for their annual vacation away from work seems like an eternity. Waiting for water to boil can sometimes seem like forever.

Waiting is like making bread. You must work hard to get the flour, the water, and the eggs mixed and then turn the dough over several times. You then place the dough in a pan, put a wet cloth over the top of it, and wait some more for the bread to rise. There is nothing you can do but wait. We wait and watch for some sign of a new beginning, like the seasons turning. Fall and winter must happen before spring and summer begin, and the cycle repeats itself.

Let's face it, we don't like to wait. In general, people are not patient. During a time of waiting, however, we have a chance to focus on growth. Waiting during tough times (such as waiting for the doctor's call with your test results, waiting for a change to occur in a relationship, or waiting to find a new job) may seem like forever. Whenever possible, we try to avoid waiting. We don't want to wait until we can afford to buy a certain item—we have to have it now. We use a credit card for instant gratification and worry about the bill later.

Here are a few basic ways that many people try to avoid waiting:

- *They try to keep moving.* Most people feel better if they're moving. They don't like to stand still and simply wait. The Disney organization seems to have this down. Notice that when you wait for admission to an attraction at Disney World, the line curves and turns, with images on the walls on TV screens to show aspects of the ride to come, and images and sounds related to the theme. All of these contextual elements are designed to take your focus off the fact that you are waiting.
- *They try to make something happen.* Inertia makes us uncomfortable. People seem to believe that they must always be doing something. I speak to groups about the loss of leisure time in the United States. I've noticed that people feel they must plan, schedule, and organize their vacations. Let's return to Disney World. What is a common question we ask someone who says he or she is going there? "Did you plan your trip?" If the answer is no, we're shocked. Most of us hate to simply let things happen.
- *They believe that life is uncertain, so they do the easy things first.* People who follow this notion often follow their statement with "So, eat dessert first." They hate to wait, to do the difficult tasks before the easy ones. Dale Carnegie said, "Do the hard jobs first. The easy jobs will take care of themselves." He became successful by working hard on the challenges and then enjoying the easy activities in life.

Do you ever feel that while you are waiting, nothing is happening? We may seem to be waiting to take the next step, but this is a false perception of waiting. While you wait, you learn to surrender and cooperate with the change that is happening around you. You can learn patience and cultivate your powers of observation. There is a value in waiting that is different from procrastination.

As a procrastinator, you can also reframe your thoughts and not view time as being wasted. The author Bertrand Russell once said, "The time you enjoy wasting is not wasted time." Enjoy your time off and do something fun with it. You are not wasting time; you are making the most of your leisure hours.

In other circumstances, when you must endure an enforced period of waiting, you can use the time productively. Jon lost his manufacturing job. His boss said that there was a very good chance that in several months he could be rehired. Jon was a good employee and had performed his job well, so he had little doubt that his boss would rehire him. He could have then spent the next eight to ten months just sitting around waiting for the call to come back to work. Instead, Jon went to the local community college and took a couple of courses to retool himself and become an even more valuable employee. He did not complain that he'd lost his job, and he did not waste his time waiting. He used his time productively.

Don't confuse procrastination with waiting. With procrastination, you are working hard *not* to have something happen. With waiting, you are preparing for the next step—you are working toward a goal, not avoiding one. Buddhists turn our view of waiting on its head when they say, "Don't just do something, sit there." I interpret this to mean using your time while you wait, to prepare for the next step. Get ready to meet the needs of your new job by taking classes, read up on the pros and cons of that medical procedure, or enhance your social skills to improve a new relationship; you could even decorate your house and leave some cookies and milk for Santa. You don't have to try to climb Mount Everest; small accomplishments are just as rewarding.

So when people tell you they are not procrastinating but instead are waiting for the next thing to happen, ask them what they are doing in the interim and how they are preparing for that next step in life. Tell them that procrastination means actively avoiding the things that need to get done. Waiting is actively preparing for things that will happen.

I ask that you don't confuse procrastination with *delaying*. There are times when delaying to make a decision or perform an action is totally appropriate. It helps us gather more information or pause to see what action is needed. That's not procrastination, because you continue after the pause. It's not irrational to wait to "gather the troops" before marching forward. Waiting or delaying is not the problem. Not starting or not finishing when it makes sense to finish—that is the problem.

Time is finite. We don't really manage time; we manage our activities within the time we have.

Focus on the Now, Then, or What Will Be

The British novelist G. B. Stein once wrote humorously, "One thing that's good about procrastination is that you always have something planned for tomorrow." Thinking about the future is not a bad thing to do. It is adaptive and healthy to consider what will occur next, to wonder whether you are prepared to handle certain situations and to figure out where you will go from here.

Reminiscing about the past can be a healthy process, or it may result in inertia—you simply can't get started. When you look back on what you have accomplished or the things you still need to do, this can help you focus on the steps you need to take next. DePaul graduate student Emily Sumner and I examined whether procrastinators, when they focus on events in their past, engage in "ruminating about failures" or "savoring the good times." Maybe as a procrastinator you can't get yourself moving forward because you repeatedly dwell on times when you made a decision or acted in a way that resulted in failure:

- The hotel that you chose for the family trip was dirty and damp.
- The washing machine you purchased without comparison shopping was more expensive than a competitor's offer.
- The DVD player you bought simply was not manufactured to standards.

On the other hand, as a procrastinator you may remember all of the good times you had, and you reminisce about them all of the time:

- That trip to the Caribbean beach house was so special, you just keep remembering it over and over again—no other vacation could match it.
- Your first family car was so durable and comfortable, you can't purchase another that will come close.
- Your boyfriend from college was so special, no other guy could match him.

In the study that Emily and I conducted, using two separate samples of adult procrastinators and nonprocrastinators, we found that rumination on negative events was more pronounced for procrastinators than was the savoring of positive events. Still, some procrastinators did savor the happy moments they recalled. They wrote about childhood and adult episodes that were personal or that involved others (they listed more than seventeen hundred past "good time moments" for their lives in only three or four minutes' time). The lesson here is that you need to live in the moment.

Living in the moment is useful. The aborigines in the Australian Outback have no word for "yesterday" and no word for "tomorrow." They live for today. Only the present is relevant in their lives. Some people today call it "going with the flow."

What can be said of your procrastination tendencies and your time perspective? Given that the ability to organize your day is at the core of timing many of your daily acts, it seems important to understand the process of time, as procrastinators see it. Many people hold the belief that procrastinators are time wasters, but it is not clear what procrastinators really think when it comes to time.

It seems that procrastinators do not focus on the future. DePaul student Mark Specter and I explored the time preferences of procrastinators (Specter and Ferrari 2000). We found that adult men and women who reported procrastinating frequently were less likely to ponder the future and more likely to focus on the past; procrastinators do not think about the present very often. In other words, as a procrastinator you focus on the past, you are less likely to focus on the future, and the present does not seem relevant to you.

Sean always seems to look to the past. He ruminates about the things he missed: the old girlfriend he failed to impress, the job that got away, the concert ticket he never purchased. Sean needs to focus on the *now* and live more in the present than in the past. He fails to savor the good times that are happening right now, and he may not even be aware of pleasant events that occur around him every day. Sean does not realize that his coworker Rachel likes him. He is too busy moping over the loss of his old girlfriend from seven years ago. Sean needs to live in the present.

In fact, on closer examination, our research determined that for some procrastinators, their time perspective was associated negatively with the present and seemed fatalistic in orientation. In a survey of Spanish-speaking adults, conducted by me and Dr. Juan Diaz-Morales of the University of Madrid, the individuals seemed to have a hopeless attitude toward the future and life in general. In contrast, the time perspective of other procrastinators was associated positively with the present but was more hedonistic, reflecting a risk-taking attitude toward time and life. All of the procrastinators perceived reflecting on the future as negative.

This research shows that procrastinators' tendency not to focus on the future is apparently a global phenomenon. Procrastinators who live in non–English speaking countries are similar to procrastinators from the United States, Britain, and Australia. More important, if you are a procrastinator, these studies reveal that you need to live in the now to achieve your goals and must learn to make the act of completing projects before their deadlines more attractive. No doubt, you will feel better in the long run if you finish current tasks instead of leaving them undone.

Dr. Sean McCrea of the University of Konstanz in Germany and his colleagues (McCrea, Liberman, Trope, and Sherman 2008) found that people procrastinate because they believe that tomorrow will be a better day to get things moving forward. According to their model, events and tasks that are in the distant future are more abstract to us, because we can't see them happening today or even tomorrow. Consequently, people procrastinate. In contrast, we focus on and complete tasks that are more concrete and that seem to be due in the near future (like tomorrow).

These results have a profound impact on helping you understand how you view life and the limited time we all have on this earth. Focusing on the past or on the distant future, without considering the present, is not adaptive. It will not help you enjoy what is happening at the moment, and you will miss the simple joys that surround you.

Feeling helpless or fatalistic about the present, as if there is nothing you can do to change your destiny, will not help you enjoy life. Instead, plan for the future. Consider your next steps. Look around you at what is happening now and see how that can help you live a more fruitful life.

Be careful, though. Some procrastinators do live for the present but merely see life as fun and a chance to take risks and live on the edge. A certain amount of fun is always necessary, but life is complicated, and we need to consider the future. What are the next steps we should take in life? Where are we going? Worrying about the future is not helpful, but ignoring it isn't the answer either. Instead, make accomplishing your current tasks an attractive goal and celebrate when you've completed them. The next time you finish your taxes before April 15, plan a party with friends.

Does the Early Bird Get the Worm?

Is there a certain time of the day that you begin tasks? Are you an early bird or a night owl? When do you prefer to get things done?

Phil loves to work on business reports at night, starting around 10 p.m. He claims that he does his best work the night before the report is due. Does this practice really result in his best work or would he be better off starting earlier and ending up with a more thorough and complete report?

Are procrastinators night or day people? Do they like to work on tasks at night, because they claim to be more alert and active in the late afternoon and evening hours, or do they prefer working in the early morning? It may not surprise you that adult procrastinators more often claim they are night people, preferring to work on social or individual activities after dark (Ferrari, Harriott, Evans, Lecik-Michna, and Wenger 1997). Four of my students and I posed that question to several hundred participants and found that procrastinators are indeed creatures of the night. As a procrastinator, you may enjoy shopping, eating out, seeing a movie, pleasure reading, exercising, spending time with friends, working on a hobby, and playing group sports—all at night.

We asked procrastinators to record in a daily diary all of the activities they worked on—including the time of day— during a six-day period (Ferrari et al. 1997). We recorded hundreds of tasks, but there was no significant difference between procrastinators and nonprocrastinators in the number or the quality of the tasks. Procrastinators, however (even those in international samples), were more likely to list their tasks as started or completed at night (cf. Diaz-Morales, Cohen, and Ferrari 2008). Procrastinators started at the last minute (at night) and reported failing to complete many of their tasks. The tasks were just "hanging there" waiting to be finished.

What would happen if you started your tasks earlier in the day? Would you fail because you started at 10 a.m. instead of 10 p.m.? For certain tasks, maybe this approach of starting late would work. But I think for most things in life, it wouldn't. It is a myth that some procrastinators need to start a task close to the deadline in order to get motivated by working against the clock. If you start a task on time, your attitude toward the job will change. Once you begin, you will discover that the task is not so bad. Researchers have found that we feel good when we make progress toward our goals. And if we are happier about our goals, we are more likely to work on them.

If you start a task and try to do it effectively within a very limited amount of time, this won't give you more time. Don't blame yourself if you can't complete it, but don't blame "lack of time" either. There are only twenty-four hours in a day and seven days in a week. You can't stretch them out to last longer, no matter how hard you try. Yet you may be amazed at how much you can accomplish in fifteen minutes. Do you have to wait in line at the post office or the bank for fifteen minutes? Write some notes, address some envelopes, or catch up on reading. Distract yourself from waiting, and you will feel less anxious about the present.

Tasks That Procrastinators Choose to Do and Try to Avoid

Let's examine the kind of tasks that procrastinators, compared to nonprocrastinators, prefer. If procrastinators were told that they either would or would not receive performance feedback after completing one of four tasks, which task would they choose?

Suppose you were presented with four envelopes, each stuffed with what you believed to be task materials and each envelope marked either A (described as an easy task and not very revealing of a person's skills), B (also easy, but more indicative of a person's skills), C (described as a difficult task to complete and not very informative about a person's skills), or D (difficult and informative). Then you were asked to choose which task you wanted to complete. You did not know that once you made your choice, the study would be over.

In our study, procrastinators, more often than nonprocrastinators, chose the easy and noninformative task (A), while nonprocrastinators more frequently chose the easy and informative task (B). More important, these choices occurred most often when participants were told that they would receive feedback on their task completion.

Dr. Dan Ariely of Duke University conducted an online study with approximately three thousand Oprah.com users. His study sounded similar to the one we had completed several years earlier. Dr. Ariely found that people seemed to drag their feet on some tasks more than on others. From a list of twelve activities (which included scheduling a doctor's appointment, paying bills, and holiday shopping), exercising and starting a diet were the two that people put off the most often, and these were followed by delaying to plan for retirement. What members of Oprah's popular Web site were telling us was that they did not want to spend time getting into shape, even though most people believe that exercising and positive diet habits can improve our lives. But those activities are hard and demanding and require us to be diligent and committed. Most people don't want to follow through on what they need to do to improve their lives.

What does this mean for you and for other procrastinators? Like everyone, you seem to prefer to work on tasks that are easy. But, as my study indicated, you also want those tasks not to reveal much about your skill level. You prefer to avoid knowing where you stand in life. This avoidance prevents you from confirming your knowledge about your skills.

Remember, you need to take chances in life. You will fail at times and at other times succeed. If you avoid learning about your skill level, this does not give you information that is essential for your growth. It only causes you to procrastinate even more and prevents you from living your life to the fullest.

Instead of focusing on a fear of failure, savor your strengths. Instead of avoiding tasks that might reveal your weaknesses, look at those experiences as ways to learn about who you are and how you can grow. No one likes to think he or she is incompetent at a certain skill (such as swimming). But if you have a chance to learn that skill (for instance, your local recreation center offers swimming lessons for a minimal fee), then by all means take advantage of the opportunity.

Recently, my wife and I had some free time, and I thought it would be nice if we engaged in a fun activity together. I used to be a good ballroom dancer, having learned it as a child from my mother and my aunts (and by going to lots of Italian family dances). But my wife never really learned how to dance the waltz, the cha-cha, or the swing. When the park district in our community offered eight classes for a total of thirty dollars, I signed us both up. We looked at the experience not as a way to fail or to highlight skills that one of us lacked. Instead, it was something we could share, learn, and have fun with.

No one wants to work on difficult tasks, myself included. Yet there is a saying, "What does not kill you makes you stronger." By understanding your limits and trying to grow beyond them, you can live a more productive and fulfilled life.

What if procrastinators and nonprocrastinators were told they could choose between two tasks, one that revealed information about their social skills or another that revealed information about their thinking (cognitive) skills? I asked that question in another experiment (Ferrari 1991). Regardless of the task that participants chose, their performance would be coded in one of two ways: (1) by a research assistant while the participant watched (so the performance score would be publicly known, at least to one other person), or (2) by having the assistant code the responses with a provided answer key. The aim was to see how public or private performance influenced the choice of the task. Which situation would you have chosen?

If you are a procrastinator, you probably would say it doesn't matter if, in private, only you know the score or if someone else is aware of it. But procrastinators do prefer the social task over the cognitive task; nonprocrastinators have no preference. Procrastinators also rate the social task as more attractive and personally important and believe that they will receive a higher personal score, even in comparison to peers (Ferrari 1991).

In short, as a procrastinator you don't want feedback about your thinking (cognitive) abilities. Instead, you want to know how social you are, and you want to strengthen your social skills. That's perfectly fine, within reason. We all want others to like us. Yet the fact that you don't want feedback isn't good because feedback helps you grow. And this even pertains to feedback about your social skills: you don't want to strengthen your social skills by hearing that you can't do something. I don't blame you—I don't like to find out that I lack certain abilities, either. But let's reframe this and look at it in another way. Instead, you could ask, "How can I strengthen my social skills?" Don't look at it as if you have a deficit. Instead, think of it as a way that you can increase and strengthen the skills you do have. Build on the positives instead of focusing on the negatives.

Suppose procrastinators and nonprocrastinators each generated a list of daily tasks that he or she had worked on during a week's time. Would their lists differ? Dr. Steve Scher and I asked that precise question in another study (Scher and Ferrari 2000). We categorized such a list, which contained more than a thousand tasks, on a number of dimensions, such as academic-related, social or individual, pleasurable, needing effort, needing skills, importance to others such as friends or family, as well as on whether the tasks were completed or not. Procrastinators delayed a lot of different tasks. This study told us that procrastinators don't seem to have a pattern regarding the tasks they delay. If you are a procrastinator, chances are that you procrastinate on many things, a lot of times, and in numerous ways. This information may not be new to you. What may be new is that you are similar to nonprocrastinators in one sense: when they occasionally delay something, they have no particular preference in what they choose to delay. In this sense, procrastinators and nonprocrastinators are alike. Yet people who procrastinate seem to delay many tasks in every area of their lives.

The tasks that procrastinators prefer to delay reveal that they want to avoid knowing what their weaknesses and strengths are. Although it is understandable that you may not want to know your limits, not knowing your strengths will negatively affect your self-perception. If you know where you are, you can see where you need to go. Change is tough, but it is an important component of living a happy and healthy life. So, don't blame the tasks themselves for your procrastination. Your life tasks are no more complicated than those of the nonprocrastinator.

One more thought on the subject of tasks and procrastination. DePaul doctoral students Chad Mason, Corey Hammer, and I asked procrastinators each to write a short essay on the recent tasks they had delayed and had not delayed. Both male and female procrastinators more often described past tasks they'd delayed as difficult, requiring effort, and unpleasant— even when the completion of the tasks would have had a positive impact on the situation at the time (Ferrari, Mason, and Hammer 2005). It is interesting that tasks that needed to be completed because they were important were nevertheless delayed. As I mentioned earlier, procrastinators tend to handicap themselves and need to learn to address difficult tasks and situations upfront.

It seems that procrastinators delay just about any task—it doesn't matter what it is. They perceive the tasks that they delay, however, as unpleasant and possibly revealing of their level of skills and abilities. They will even delay tasks that are important to complete. What we see is avoidance—of the self. Procrastinators don't want to learn that they are not as capable as they think they are; they don't want others to learn that they lack certain abilities. Procrastinators even seem to sabotage themselves by not finishing important tasks that require completion. Does this sound like you?

Focus on the tasks you must complete, and work on them. Remember, priorities change, so the task may not be as important today as it was six years, six months, or even six weeks ago. Don't project your sense of insecurities onto the task, by saying that the task is boring or difficult, thereby not needing to be completed.

Dr. John Perry of Stanford University calls this strategy *structured procrastination*. He suggests that procrastinators make a list of all that needs to be done and then place the things that absolutely must get done at the top of the list. Focus on the most important and pressing tasks. But here is the trick: do all of the other items on the list. You may be surprised to see that the number one task was really not the most pressing.

It comes down to staying focused—work on the task a little at a time. Tasks are easier when you break them down into smaller, more digestible parts. For example, if writing a paper has five or six major steps, then focus on each step separately. Make an outline; gather information for parts of the outline; organize your notes into a sentence format, filling in the outline; write a rough draft; have a friend review the draft; and write the final draft, based on the edits. As another example, focus on cleaning the garage. First, organize your stuff and decide what you want to keep and what should be thrown out, things you can find a place for in the house, and items to take to a more permanent storage place. Next, go through those piles, asking yourself, "Did I use this in the last six months? Will I need this in the next six months?" Then give things that you don't need to charity—you may get a tax deduction for the contribution.

I suggest that you devise a system. So many people and companies simply don't follow a system for getting things done. Imagine that you phone a large company such as LL Bean. No matter what you order, the company has a system for filling that order. The service rep has a specific way of completing the order. The packer and the shipper in the warehouse all have a method of moving the order out and getting it into the mail.

Create a system in your life, and follow it. Do I want you to be a robot? Of course not—merely create a system, a process that allows you to get things done. For example, I can always find my car keys because whenever I walk into my house, I put them on the hook behind the front door. Sure, a few times I've misplaced the keys. And unfortunately, the kids don't always follow my system, and the keys end up somewhere else. But then we find the keys and return to the system. There is nothing wrong with organization.

Remember, your performance on the task will *not* reflect how good a person you are. Your self-worth is not tied to how well you perform. You are you, with all of your idiosyncrasies. You are not perfect, nor should you strive to be. You can learn from failure, so don't be afraid to fail.

The Three R's of Procrastination: Reactance, Revenge, and Regret

Anger is the only thing to put off till tomorrow.

—SLOVAKIAN PROVERB

Procrastination usually results in sorrowful
regret. Today's duties put off until tomorrow
gives us a double burden to bear; the best way
is to do them in their proper time.

—IDA SCOTT TAYLOR

Do the hard jobs first. The easy jobs will take
care of themselves.

—DALE CARNEGIE

Okay, you're angry—very angry. How dare they! They are not simply asking you to do something, they are *telling* you to do it. You feel as if you have no control of the situation, of your decision whether to acquiesce to their demand, no control over your actions.

I don't know your past, but I know how miserable your future will be unless you learn to deal with your anger. You can't alter yesterday, but you can manage your reactions to yesterday. The past can't be changed, but your reactions to the past are under your control.

Many procrastinators overreact and/or use revenge to deal with their anger, and others do nothing worthwhile with their anger and suffer through lives of regret. Some psychologists label the tendency to overreact in a violent way *reactance*: reacting against pressure to engage in a task. Social psychologists report that reactance occurs when a person feels that his or her personal control and freedom are taken away. In this chapter, I will discuss these three ways of dealing with anger.

"Sorry I'm Late": Apology or Apathy?

In chapter 7, I mentioned that meetings are major time suckers in the business world. It seems as if everyone has something to say, but most people are merely repeating what someone else said earlier in the meeting.

Another frustrating occurrence is when people show up late for the beginning of the meeting. I've noticed that if someone shows up two or three minutes after the announced starting time, no one seems to be upset or pay much attention. Even when a person is five or seven minutes late, the latecomer does not seem upset or embarrassed. But if you show up twenty minutes late and everyone is looking at you, you will feel embarrassed. If you arrive thirty minutes late, you really should stand in the hall! It seems you have violated a pretty serious, if unspoken, social norm.

When people arrive late, we often hear, "I'm sorry I'm late." But are they truly sorry? If they really were, does that mean they won't be late for the next meeting? The person offers an apology. Yet if we look closely, we find that this person is often late for many meetings, regardless of the topic. This makes me wonder whether the apology is sincere or merely an empty, apathetic response. After all, the latecomer's office is just down the hall from where the meeting will take place.

In fact, we could ask ourselves whether the person arrives late as a means of expressing reactance. Maybe the individual is thinking, "How dare you ask for a meeting when I am so busy—imposing your need for discussion on me when I have more important things to do? Well, I'm doing my projects first, before I go to your silly meeting."

The latecomer to the meeting may even be getting revenge against you and others at the meeting by arriving late. Perhaps the individual perceived past meetings or interactions to be unfavorable to himself or herself. In other words, the person felt hurt by something that occurred and, by being late for future meetings, can get back at the group for not respecting him or her. Some people do procrastinate as a way to get revenge.

Do latecomers feel regret from being late? That is possible; certain individuals may be offering a true apology for

their lateness. I find that latecomers who are sincerely regretful repeat that "Sorry for being late" message later in the
meeting, when they realize that they missed hearing a bit
of positive news related to them ("Oh, wow, now I'm really
sorry for coming late and missing that"). In this chapter, I'll
talk about procrastination that is motivated by reactance,
revenge, and regret.

Reactance: "Oh, Yeah? Just for That I Won't Do It!"

Don't pressure Ashley to do anything. She's usually easy-
going and open to the suggestions of others. But if you tell
her, "Do this," she will say, "Oh, yeah? Well, I was going to
do it, but now that you tell me I *must* do it, I'm not going
to." Ashley says that she feels pressured into responding and
does not want to feel confined. Even with an act that she
would have wanted to do, she has to rebel against it because
she now feels that an external pressure is "making" her act,
and she does not like it. Ashley thus overreacts against others' demands, believing that her personal freedom has been
disregarded.

How should Ashley respond? There are probably three different options:

1. She could go along with the "demand," as she sees it. She
   was going to do the task anyway; so what if someone else
   tells her to do it?
2. She could react with open aggression, yelling and throw-
   ing things at the person. She could express her anger over
   being told what to do.
3. She could (as she usually does) use reactance.

In this situation, procrastination—not responding—occurs as a result of reactance. As a procrastinator, you may see yourself as being similar to Ashley. You may even think that she is right and her actions are justified. Heck, who has the right to tell you what to do?

Life is full of situations where we must meet the demands of external forces. We must meet deadlines that we don't impose or create, such as:

Taxes
Bill paying
Holiday shopping
Anniversaries
Birthdays
Jury duty

These are only a few of the common life situations where deadlines are imposed, not only on you but on most people. Deadlines exist, they are real, they must be met. And as a procrastinator, you can meet them. Don't dwell on one negative incident all day. Don't let something that happened in the morning ruin your entire day. And don't let what happened yesterday or last week consume you. Let bygones be bygones.

I guess I'm lucky, because whenever I'm upset with things at work, I can simply walk into the classroom and turn it all off for the next hour, ninety minutes, or three hours. And when the class ends, I think back on the situation that upset me and either I let it go—or I realize I've forgotten what it was all about!

The Families and Work Institute in the United States estimates that one-third of all U.S. employees are chronically overworked (October 2008). The institute notes that 39 percent of employees experience high overwork levels and feel very angry toward their employers. This feeling of anger may trigger reactance among employees, prompting them to say, "Oh, yeah, you want me to work overtime tonight without giving me any choice in the matter? Well, then I'll just take my good old time about doing the work."

A study by global management consultancy Hay Group titled "The Loyalty Deficit" reported in October 2009 that many British workers (from a survey sample of one thousand workers) voluntarily put in an extra six hours—almost a full day—per week of unpaid overtime. Survey participants were from both public and private companies. Many of these British employees were so unhappy in their jobs that they hoped to find new jobs as soon as possible. The survey said that the extra demands placed on the workers were causing a breakdown of trust and commitment between employers and employees. Overworked and underpaid. Underappreciated and overextended. Reactance is brewing here.

It might be better for employers to lessen such employee reactance by playing an active role in their workers' lives. For instance, the employer might provide on-site day care centers, concierge services, and referrals for professional resources. Moreover, the employer could emphasize flexible scheduling, by offering employees flex-time, job sharing, telecommuting, and other arrangements that would allow them to handle personal and family problems on their own time. Solutions exist to reduce or even prevent procrastination reactance.

Procrastination reactance has a negative impact on people's lives. Reactance behavior often alienates others and pushes them away. Reactance makes us focus on the self. It becomes "all about me." You feel crossed by others. You feel that your freedom has been taken away. You feel cornered and pressured to do it their way.

No one likes a person who is difficult and not a team player. It does you no good to be angry and to use procrastination as a reactance strategy. You will distance yourself from others, and someday you may need them to help you. Someday, you may be the one placing a demand on them. Instead of using procrastination, use your skills to talk to others in a friendly and approachable manner. Try to understand why they need that task done now, and attempt to meet their needs. Then, in the future, they will be more receptive when you ask (or maybe tell) them to do something for you.

Taking Revenge the Passive/Aggressive Way

You may know someone like Walter. He delays getting important things done, shows up late for appointments and events, and generally tends to be slow in doing whatever the task or the event may need. People around Walter wonder whether he is being passive-aggressive. That is, perhaps he is displaying anger toward others by *not* responding. For Walter, using procrastination is a subtle way to express his anger toward others.

Whenever Walter feels angry at someone, he procrastinates as a form of revenge. He delays being timely when he believes others have "done me wrong." For Walter, procrastination is a form of passive-aggression that originated as a way to seek revenge on others.

The procrastination-revenge link has been explored (Ferrari and Emmons 1994). Procrastination among adult men and women is related to revenge seeking. It seems that procrastination and revenge are linked by a belief that the world is not fair and just, so revenge is needed to make things right.

Many people believe that in life you get what you deserve, and you deserve what you get. They believe the world is fair and just. Social psychologists call that the "Just World Belief." Persons with a strong BJW concept (that's short for "belief in a just world") see the world as always needing to be equitable. They live with the idea that good things happen to good people. If that is true, then when life gives you unfair challenges or you get blamed for something you did not do, are you a bad person? I don't think so.

Instead, I believe that people are neither good nor bad—they are people. And our actions are not good or bad, they are actions. Those actions may be appropriate or inappropriate ways to respond. The world is not just and fair—it is the world.

So, why use revenge to get even? Dr. Emmons and I found that some procrastinators use revenge as a way to seek justice in life (Ferrari and Emmons 1994). In that study, we asked more than two hundred men and women to report on their tendencies to procrastinate and to complete surveys on aspects of their personalities, such as a desire to seek revenge. We found that the more a person seeks revenge in life, the more he or she procrastinates. Because this was a correlational study, one could interpret our results in the other direction—the more a person procrastinates, the more he or she seeks revenge in life. We can't say whether revenge causes procrastination or procrastination causes revenge. But we can say that procrastination and revenge are associated behaviors in some people.

Maybe, you believe (as Walter, who was described earler, does) that by procrastinating, you'll get even with the person and there will be some justice in this situation. Revenge is the result of holding onto a grudge, and the feelings of anger will eat away at you. This anger will consume you until you cannot experience the joys in life. It will make you focus completely on yourself. But the world is *not* about you—it is about us. We live with others; we must include others in our lives. Revenge makes us see the world as if only the self matters.

Life, unfortunately, is not fair. Things happen that we cannot control, and we must do the best we can. I'm not saying to accept mediocrity or fate. Instead, I believe that you shape your future and your destiny. By engaging in life in constructive ways, such as not procrastinating, you win people over more effectively than by seeking revenge. It takes too much energy to strategically plot a course of revenge. Instead, focus on what you can control and work with others in areas where you have limited power.

Don't always take yourself or others so seriously. Cultivate the ability to laugh at yourself. Nobody's perfect all of the time. As I said earlier, even Mary Poppins was only "practically perfect." Not everything you do will be a masterpiece, so don't seek revenge for the mistakes that happen in life. Instead, find humor in your mistakes. You might become your own best source of entertainment.

The great golf professional Arnold Palmer said, "The road to success is always under construction." You are a continuing work of art. Don't waste energy or time on revenge. Don't focus on yourself so much. Show others signs of appreciation, give credit where credit is due, and focus on how you can help others succeed.

Are Your Regrets Too Few or Too Many to Mention?

It's a true story, it's a common story—a story of derailed dreams. It's a story of high hopes colliding with harsh realities. It's a story of regret. Many people live with a lifetime of regrets.

Bob could have gone to college on a soccer scholarship. It was offered to him right out of high school. Instead, he joined a rock-and-roll band and now has a dead-end job fixing garage doors. "Now I'm stuck," he said. His dreams were derailed.

Pick up any high school yearbook, and you'll see this question asked of seniors: "What do you plan to do with your life after graduation?" The answers that follow are stories of travel, adventure, civic duty, and social justice. Now fast-forward twenty years to the Class of XXXX, High School Reunion. Some dreams came true, but many dreams did not. How many of those adults feel a sense of regret? Changing directions in life is not tragic. Losing passion in life is tragic.

The legendary singer Frank Sinatra's "My Way" is a classic. In this song, which Sinatra sang toward the end of his career, he notes that he may have regrets in life but "too few to mention." In his life, he did it his way. He lived life to the fullest, and when reminiscing on the past, he savored the good times and did not ruminate about the bad times.

Don't focus on what did not happen and why it didn't go the way you planned. Like reactance and revenge, regret is *self*-focus. You are thinking all about yourself and not about others. You are seeing the world as "all about me," instead of "all about we." Regret will freeze your heart and will prevent you from moving forward. As a procrastinator, do you have many or few regrets in life?

Kelly Barnes, an undergraduate from Trinity Christian University who joined my research team at DePaul, along with Dr. Piers Steel of the University of Calgary and I, surveyed more than four thousand adult men and women on their procrastination tendencies and feelings of regret across twelve life domains. Our study shows that feelings of regret are common (Ferrari, Barnes, and Steel 2009). The situations that provoked regretful feelings included missed career opportunities, not engaging in community volunteer services, educational status and degrees, parenting interactions, time spent with family, financial planning, interacting with one's friends, taking care of one's health, spending time on leisure activities, missed romances, spiritual growth and development, and personal growth opportunities.

Compared to nonprocrastinators, both men and women procrastinators reported greater feelings of regret over missed educational opportunities and not seeking the best or highest education they could obtain, missed opportunities to share events with family and friends, not engaging in physical exercise or dieting in order to have healthy lives, and inadequate financial planning for their future. There were no significant differences in the degree of regret that procrastinators compared to nonprocrastinators felt about their career choices, romantic involvement, spiritual growth, and personal development.

I wonder whether Sinatra had regrets in any of these areas when he said his feelings of remorse were "too few to mention."

You Can Either Live the Sorrowful Life or Express Your Creative Soul

Author Ida Scott Taylor's quote at the beginning of this chapter captures the role of regret in procrastinating. It does not serve you well to engage in "sorrowful regret." Why lament about what could not be done? Instead, focus on "gettin' dun," as I mentioned earlier. Focus on accomplishing your goals. There is no need to apologize for trying; it is in *not* trying that we fail.

You can accomplish more than you think when you focus on the task and not on the feelings of remorse that may arise. We spend too much time trying to discern what others think of us. The late Carnegie Mellon professor Randy Pausch, in his 2008 book *The Last Lecture*, said that we spend so much time figuring out what others think of us that we deplete our resources for being creative. Dr. Pausch was direct with his students so that they knew where they stood—what their strengths and weaknesses were—which enabled them to soar to new, unexplored heights.

Procrastinators need to focus less on what others think of them, pay more attention to what must get done, and then do the best that they can. If you find yourself late to the start of a project or a meeting or perhaps you've missed a deadline, then do some self-reflection. Ask yourself—am I angry now, and why? Will this anger get the job done? Is it justified? Does this person really deserve my anger? At the opening of this chapter, I think the Slovakian proverb is well worth repeating, if you are someone who experiences reactance and expresses revenge through procrastination: "Anger is the only thing to put off till tomorrow."

"It's always darkest before the dawn" is a phrase I've often heard. Give your anger until tomorrow—think it through and then let it go. Reactance against others' deadlines or getting revenge by not meeting deadlines will not work. Maybe when someone tells you directly that he or she does not like something you've done, you should accept it, rather than get angry and indulge in reactance or seek revenge. You should consider the criticism to be helpful feedback that will enable you to grow. If you overreact, you may feel regret. And if this becomes your lifestyle, you may have regrets in the future—too many to mention.

Social Support: Getting By with a Little Help from My Friends

Begin while others are procrastinating.
Work while others are wishing.

—WILLIAM ARTHUR WARD

———————————

You may delay, but time will not.

—BENJAMIN FRANKLIN

At the end of the famous Oscar-winning movie *Gone with the Wind*, the lead female character on whom the story is focused, Scarlett O'Hara, is upset. Her husband and the only man who really, truly understood her, Rhett Butler, is leaving—for the last time. As he walks away from her, through the front door and into the night mist and fog, Scarlett asks Rhett, "What shall I do? Where shall I go?" His answer is the classic line "Frankly, my dear, I don't give a damn." But Scarlett's reaction at this moment is the classic procrastinator's response to such troubles and conflicts: "I'll worry about it tomorrow, for tomorrow is another day."

Scarlett is entering a life of transition. She needs to grow up and assume more personal responsibility for her life. Transitions are hard, challenging, and often painful. In transitions, we move from the end of one situation to the beginning of something new. That transition period may be confusing because we don't know how to act, what to do, or where to go next. The old techniques for coping that we used in the past may not work for the next set of situations. Transitions entail something ending or dying and something new emerging.

But change is a challenge. Sometimes we are in denial that our old ways of acting simply don't work anymore. So, what do we focus on—our past behavior (which is known and convenient and safe but is no longer effective) or the new beginnings (by challenging ourselves to live life differently)?

In a transition, you are being asked to stop delaying and stop using the familiar blaming techniques and thoughts you found comforting in the past. Instead, you must change to a new way of thinking, acting, and feeling. You don't need to please everyone all of the time, in every way. You need to live life more fully.

Consider this possibility: "What if I were kicked off my horse?" That is, suppose you are riding a horse and the horse refuses to go the way you want to go, so it throws you or kicks you off as you ride. Instead of trying to fight against the horse's different directions, suppose you let the horse (life, if you will) kick you out of your comfort zone. Now, you must make a change. You can't get back on that same horse. Instead, you must transition to a new phase in life with new skills. Or perhaps the process is more gentle, and you gradually come to the conclusion that now is the time to get off the horse so that you can live life more fully. You decide that you need to stop procrastinating.

In this book, I've discussed the nature of procrastination and suggested ways that people can learn new ways of coping, while adjusting to a life as a nonprocrastinator. Let's consider a few social and mutual support strategies.

When Your Life Is in Transition, Seek Circles of Support

The transition from procrastinating as a lifestyle to nonprocrastinating may be a painful period. But why focus either on the end of one phase of life or on a transition that can involve growing pains? To stop being a procrastinator, focus on the beginning of your new life. Think about the abundance you will gain from not procrastinating.

Living through a transition is a challenge, and you can't make it alone. You need social support and circles of friends to help you grow. As a procrastinator, you need to find others who will be supportive of your desire to change, who value you as a person with strengths and weaknesses. The supportive communities you engage can help you focus on new ways to act and to think. Your judgment during a transition may be clouded or may need direction. Supportive communities act as sounding boards; you can bounce ideas off them, they can help you clarify your thoughts, and they can act as effective role models.

Just as everyone needs support from, and approval by, others, so do procrastinators. When you need others' help, such as empathy when you lose a job or a close relationship ends or you simply want someone to listen to your fears and worries, it's natural to turn to other people.

Scarlett O'Hara was upset because the only person in her support system, Rhett Butler, would no longer be present to guide her when she felt lost, to help her when she needed strength, and to cheer her up when she felt gloomy. Her support system was gone.

I suggest that you use your social support systems to stop procrastinating. Make an agreement with a friend or a family member to ensure that you don't skip out of the task at hand. For instance, as the procrastinator in the relationship, you can tell your friend that he should not join you for a dinner out until you accomplish writing eight pages of your class assignment. Ask your friend to insist that you show him those eight written pages outside the entrance of the restaurant. If you don't have the pages, then your friend should go home. And tell your friend not to accept any excuses from you, either.

Dorothy, in the movie *The Wizard of Oz*, cannot make the transition from her black-and-white world of Kansas to the colors of the rainbow in the Land of Oz without the social support, guidance, assistance, and suggestions of Scarecrow, Tin Man, and Cowardly Lion. When she returns home to Kansas at the end of the movie, the setting is still black and white, but Dorothy has changed, having become wiser and more skilled in life. The journey was a challenge, but the start of her new life is amazing. As a procrastinator, don't you need the help of others to change?

Within the social and behavioral sciences, the concepts of social and mutual support are used interchangeably. For clarification, however, social support is broader, reflecting assistance given to others usually when they need to cope with stressors. Scientists and therapists agree that seeking social support when in crisis, when dealing with loss, and when looking for direction in life are signs of healthy, adaptive living. Helping professionals also talk about the need for social support when individuals experience times of crises.

More recently, scientists and practitioners have coined the term *mutual support*, to imply a reciprocal responsibility to receive and give support. With mutual support, there is an implicit assumption that each person helps the other. Unlike formal therapy, however, where experts provide "top-down" guidance, mutual support involves no trained professionals but simply ordinary people helping other people.

Some good examples of supportive mutual help settings are 12-step recovery programs. Here, each member of the group provides support, insight, advice, and guidance to other members of the group. Each person is like a mentor to the others. The members share a common mission or goal, and there is a reciprocal process of helping among members.

The members of 12-step programs also share their life stories. They talk about the process of change they go through—the pitfalls, the setbacks, the obstacles. And they tell others when they succeed, experience growth, and make transitions.

Regardless of the term, I want to discuss procrastination and social or mutual support. It is normal and healthy for you to seek support and comfort from others. This is a very human process and need. It is okay to ask for help, to seek help, to look for support from others. It is okay to let your life unfold in public as you make the transition from a lifestyle of procrastination.

The Buck Stops Here

Procrastinators need others to help them deal with challenges in life, as everyone else does. You must be careful, however, because as a procrastinator you tend to let other people do things for you. Procrastinators allow others to bail them out of trouble. Some social and behavioral scientists call this buck passing, the tendency to simply let others do whatever needs to be done.

You may be familiar with this quote from President Harry Truman: "The buck stops here." When Truman became president, he announced that the changes (transitions) that would occur during his term would be his responsibility, whether successful or not. Even the president of the United States knew that we could not continue to blame others for our problems; we had to take responsibility, satisfy our needs, and meet our goals. We all have a responsibility to get things done, and even though others may provide us with guidance and direction, ultimately we must confront the challenges in our lives.

President John F. Kennedy knew this as well. Consider the Bay of Pigs invasion of Cuba, when hundreds of Cuban exiles left Miami, Florida, to cross over the seas and invade dictator

Fidel Castro's country. Kennedy was aware of the plan and was supported by the CIA. When it was discovered the morning after the failed invasion by the Cuban exiles that Kennedy had refused to offer U.S. air support to protect the invaders, he had a choice. Kennedy could have said he did not know about the plan (which was originally conceived by President Dwight D. Eisenhower, his predecessor, just before the start of his term), or he could assume responsibility. Kennedy assumed responsibility for the disaster.

Americans were impressed. A president admitted his mistake—a major mistake with serious consequences. And, in turn, Americans gave a high approval rating to this new leader.

If these two presidents of the United States could admit that they'd made mistakes, that they were responsible for their actions, and that the "buck stops here," then why do we find it hard to admit we are wrong? Why do procrastinators prefer to pass the buck?

Consider the following situation—it might be common in your life. It's 7:30 p.m., and you have just finished eating a wonderful dinner with your partner. The dinner prep required lots of pots and pans and fancy table settings, and considerable piles of dishes now need washing. Your partner is not a procrastinator, so he gets up and says to you that he will wash the dinner dishes and pots.

But you say to your nonprocrastinating partner, "No, I'll do them later." He agrees. I predict that this is what likely occurs: The evening progresses from 7:30 to 8:45 without the dishes being washed. Then it is 9:20 and the pile is still there. You look at the clock, and now it is 10:35. Nothing has moved from the sink. Now it is 11:30, and your partner wants to go to bed. You and your partner know that the sink needs to be cleared of the dishes and the pans washed. So your partner goes into the kitchen and bails you out from procrastinating by washing the dishes. As he does the next-to-last pot or pan, you come over and say, "Oh, I was going to do them."

Can you imagine how your partner feels at that time— angry? Disappointed? Sure—but he bailed you out. The buck did not stop with you. You did not do the dishes. Someone else had to do the task that you assumed the responsibility for.

Do You Confide in Family or Friends in Times of Trouble?

Procrastinators report that they are what research and clinical psychologists call *interpersonally dependent*, meaning that they will let other people (a spouse, a friend, a family member) do tasks for them. They protect their self-esteem by letting other people do the work. I found that among adult men and women procrastinators, more than among nonprocrastinators, the tendency to let others do the tasks that need to be done is common (Ferrari 1994). In fact, with adults from Spain and the United States, Dr. Juan Diaz-Morales, of the University of Madrid, Spain, and I found that procrastinators presented a public image of helplessness and neediness (Ferrari and Diaz-Morales 2007b). When questioned whether they let others do tasks for them, the procrastinators, more than nonprocrastinators, responded they were interpersonally dependent. Why?

If the task is not successfully completed, it isn't the fault of the procrastinator because he or she didn't do it. "I did not make the decision." "I did not do it." The procrastinator avoids blame. If the task is done well, however, the procrastinator can bask in the glory of the accomplished task. Either way, the procrastinator ends up looking good and feeling pleased with himself or herself.

But the procrastinator's relationship with the nonprocrastinator might suffer. The nonprocrastinator goes beyond the role of offering support, crossing the boundary to actually doing the task for the procrastinator. In turn, the nonprocrastinator may feel cheated, used, as if he or she is the "slave" of the procrastinator.

In the previous example of washing dishes, if the dishes are not cleaned to a high standard, the procrastinator can avoid feeling that it was his or her fault, because that person did not do the washing. If the dishes *are* washed well, then everyone can use the clean dishes.

I don't mean to assign blame to you, for buck passing. Instead, I want you to work with others to get tasks done. Use your supportive communities to help you make the transition into a life of nonprocrastination. You don't need to let others bail you out of difficult situations or even easy tasks. It is a mutual relationship, where sometimes you do certain tasks, and other times they do them. You can achieve happiness by accomplishing the tasks you are responsible for. Focus on how much more mutually enjoyable the relationship will be when you become a nonprocrastinator.

To whom do procrastinators turn for social support when they are in need of approval? When they're depressed? Angry? Frustrated? Do procrastinators seek social support from family or friends? That was the question DePaul University doctoral student Jesse Harriott and undergraduate Maureen Zimmerman and I asked in a research study of women and men (Ferrari, Harriott, and Zimmerman 1999). In this study, participants listed all of the acquaintances, friends, and best friends they could think of in ten minutes. Next, participants assessed the quality of their relationships with their parents, as well as their best male and best female friends, identified from among their self-generated lists.

What we found was that both procrastinators and nonpro-crastinators have similar-size social networks. Procrastinators and nonprocrastinators generated the same number of acquaintances, friends, and best friends. That is good news—nonprocrastinators are not so task-oriented that they don't have friends. And procrastinators have a large enough net-work of friends who can help them transition away from a lifestyle of delaying.

It is good for you to realize that your social support net-work is not small or unusual, compared to nonprocrastinators' networks. It is composed of the same types of relationships with roughly the same number of people you can count on in times of trouble. But the quality of procrastinators' relation-ships differed from those of nonprocrastinators. In a variety of situations where people needed help, procrastinators said that they seek social support from friends; nonprocrastinators seek support from family members.

Procrastinators said that they have more tension and con-flicts with their parents and with their same-sex best friends, compared to nonprocrastinators. Now, this makes sense. Who knows you best—your best friend and your close family mem-bers or your more casual friends? The answer is your family and your best friend. They have been with you for years—they know about your successes and failures in life. Your best friend and your family were there to recall the other times in your life when your procrastination caused you to miss an important event, submit an incomplete or inaccurate application, or miss other opportunities.

I also found that procrastinators, more than nonprocras-tinators, mentioned that they had conflicts and arguments with their best friends more than with their more casual friends. Again, think about that. Your best friend, like your parents, has a history with you. She knows your life, and she knows you. So when you procrastinate, she recalls the other times when those intentional delays were costly. And frankly, as a procrastinator you don't want to remember those failures. You don't want someone like your mother or father or best friend to remind you of how those tendencies to intentionally delay have negatively affected on your life. As a result, interpersonal conflict occurs between you and those closest to you.

If you are a procrastinator and you failed at something because of your delaying tactics, your parents and best friends may be quick to tell you that the reason was that you never got around to beginning or completing the task. Procrastinators don't want to be reminded that they failed— to hear that they might not have taken responsibility for their actions. They don't want to hear that they must let the "buck stop here." They would rather let others be responsible for getting tasks done.

Best friends, much like your parents, also know a lot about your life history. They were around in social settings and on occasions that your parents might not have witnessed. Your best friends witnessed the fallout from your frequent procrastination. Yet even though your best friends remember your failures, they are still your friends and your support network.

Procrastinators turn to more casual friends, then, for the sympathy and understanding they need. For example, take a look at these situations:

- *You lost a job.* Casual friends say, "Oh that's terrible. You are right—they treated you poorly at that job. It's better that they let you go." A family member or your best friend says, "Well, there you go again, if only you had gotten the work done when you were asked."

- *A relationship ends.* Casual friends say, "Oh, it was terrible the way you were treated. You know, he was no good for you anyway, so ending this relationship is the best thing for you." A family member or your best friend says, "You can't hold down a relationship because you are always late, and it frustrates people."

Which would you rather hear? Of course, you prefer sympathy from casual friends over the blunt honesty of your best friend or your parents. Why take ownership for one's shortcomings, when we can let others bail us out of trouble?

Yet learning to deal with procrastination means taking ownership of your strengths and your weaknesses. Change occurs when you realize that you must conquer your challenges. The buck stops with you, when *you* take ownership for what needs to be changed. Don't blame others; don't blame yourself—just take ownership of your life and move forward.

Learn, as Scarlett O'Hara did, to make the transition from seeing the world as focused on you and your needs. Tomorrow is another day—but it is a new day to live life as a nonprocrastinator. The role models and the supportive communities will help you survive the burning Atlanta of your life and become a nonprocrastinator.

Learn, as Dorothy did in Oz, to travel through life with your friends. Like Dorothy, you alone are wearing the ruby slippers of success. You alone must find your way home to a life of nonprocrastination. You're not in Kansas anymore.

Include your friends, as well as your family, as you make the transition to a life with much less procrastination. Your parents, siblings, and best friends are here to support you. They love you and want you to enjoy life to the fullest.

How Coworkers Evaluate Peer Procrastinators

There is another point to be made related to social networks, social support communities, and procrastination. How do others view procrastinators? How are those perceptions affected if the observer is also a procrastinator?

In the corporate and working world, chronic procrastinators evaluate other procrastinators harshly, even if the procrastinators label themselves "perfectionists" to explain why they are slow to complete tasks. Others view procrastinators as the reason for a project's or a company's failure and feel that these people should be fired from their jobs.

In 2004, DePaul University undergraduate student Tina Patel and I conducted a study to examine the social comparisons between procrastinators and nonprocrastinators (Ferrari and Patel 2004). Participants rated another person as similar or different from themselves when that individual acted as a procrastinator or a nonprocrastinator. Women and men who self-identified as procrastinators or nonprocrastinators read a fictional but realistic conversation between Chris and Pat (generic names were used, in order not to suggest any gender bias). The conversation was either about a social event (buying tickets to a concert and seeking employment for a summer job) or a cognitive decision (choosing a class for the next quarter and deciding on a gift to purchase).

Results showed that both procrastinators and nonprocrastinators rated Pat (the procrastinator in the conversation story) harshly and stated that they did not like this person. Chris (the nonprocrastinator) was evaluated more positively.

Let's say that again, in another way—procrastinators said they would not want to be friends with a similar peer, someone who was a procrastinator like themselves. They could not rely on this person for their social support system, even though they themselves were procrastinators, like Pat. This study tells us that procrastinators don't think fondly of others who procrastinate. When they want social or mutual support, procrastinators may turn to their friends for comfort, but if that friend is also a procrastinator, the person seeking comfort will not like the other procrastinator very much.

That is an important piece of information for you. Your friends will be your support system when you need comfort and guidance. That's a good thing. And it is encouraged that you seek support from your family members as well. They are your closest relatives. But you must realize that if your supportive community (friends or family) consists mostly of procrastinators like you, then it is very likely that they won't value your habit of being late, of procrastinating. Instead, procrastinators seem to prefer people who are not procrastinators.

If you have lots of friends who also procrastinate frequently, they may not be as supportive of you as you think. It is possible that these "peer procrastinators" want to distance themselves from you. They don't want to associate with someone who is similar to them in tardiness.

This study suggests that you seek nonprocrastinators in your network of friends as you make the transition away from your lifestyle of frequently delaying. Besides offering support and understanding, nonprocrastinator friends may provide guidance on how to be more successful. They may be mentors for any change you seek and role models for how you should act in life.

Procrastinators Are Viewed as Social Loafers

Dr. Tim Pychyl from Carleton University and I conducted an unpublished study that found that procrastinators are viewed by others as social loafers (Ferrari and Pychyl 2008). Social loafers are people who, when given a chance in a group assignment to slack off and not work as hard as others, will choose to do little or no work. This effect emerges when the social loafer is not going to be singled out for his or her performance. For example, social loafing occurs when group grades are given for classroom tasks, and no one individual will get a grade that is different from anyone else in the group, even if one person does more work than the others do.

Ron works in a small group with four other colleagues in his office. They are a product production team, and together they must market and craft specific products. Ron is likable in many ways, but he is a social loafer. When working in this group on quarterly and monthly reports, he lets the others take the lead and do the bulk of the assignments. Although he doesn't boast or try to take sole credit for group accomplishments, he does let the work be done by others in the group.

If you asked Ron's peers what they thought of his job performance, I suspect that they would rate him low. They may like him as a person in the office, because he is friendly, but they don't like his social loafing when it comes to doing tasks. Peers do not like social loafers who procrastinate.

Group members perceive procrastinators as social loafers when they are working together on a task. In other words, even in group settings procrastinators are judged harshly. In turn, they may not be able to count on other procrastinators for support or help.

When you are working on a team project (at home, at school, or at the office), I suggest that you step up to the plate and become engaged. You will be respected by the team. Yes, even if you fail and your efforts are not perfect, the group will respect the fact that you tried. You will not fail all of the time.

Many of your efforts will be successful. And at least you tried to accomplish your goals.

When Scarlett O'Hara's sister-in-law is close to death after a difficult childbirth, the woman does not blame Scarlett for not finding a doctor in time among the ruins of Atlanta. Instead, she thanks her for doing her best.

When Scarecrow tries to stop the Wicked Witch from hurting his friends Dorothy, Tin Man, and Lion but, in turn, catches on fire, his friends thank him for his efforts.

Don't pass the buck when something needs to be done. Moreover, accomplish your tasks in a timely manner. Remember, your efforts affect others, and if you are unable to finish a task on time, then others will not be able to complete their assignments. Life is a chain of events and situations, and each person we meet in life is on our team and a link in our chain. The chain is strong when all of the links are tight and firmly connected.

Dealing with Others in Social Settings: A Summary

In regard to social support communities, procrastinators tend to let others do things for them. That's called interpersonal dependency. Procrastinators also turn to their casual friends more than to their family or best friends for social support in times of trouble. This is so because they want sympathy instead of the brutal honesty that their family and best friends will give them. Chronic procrastinators don't favor or approve of other procrastinators. In situations where a group is assigned to complete a task, procrastinators are viewed as social loafers or slackers, even by other procrastinators.

You don't have to be alone in making a transition to a happier life. Use your supportive communities to cultivate new skills and strategies. Take control of your life and focus on a new beginning—a life without procrastination. Take ownership of situations and tasks in your life—let the "buck stop here, now" with you. You can do it and do it well.

Take the reins of your "life horse," if you stay astride it, and direct it to the goals you set. If the horse kicks you off, use this as a positive opportunity to grow and make the transition to a more productive and happier life. If you decide to get off the horse because it's heading in the wrong direction, then move forward on your own as you focus on your new life of nonprocrastination.

Academic Procrastination: Why Students Delay, and How It Affects the Rest of Their Lives

Procrastination is the bad habit of putting off
until the day after tomorrow what should have
been done the day before yesterday.

—NAPOLEON HILL, AUTHOR AND ADVISER TO

FRANKLIN ROOSEVELT

How soon "not now" becomes "never."

—MARTIN LUTHER

cademic procrastination is maladaptive, yet common. Why? This whole book could be devoted to the topic of academic procrastination—but, fortunately, a very good one already exists and provides an in-depth analysis (Schouwenburg, Lay, Pychyl, and Ferrari 2004). It is a scholarly text published by the American Psychological Association, titled *Counseling the Procrastinator in Academic Settings*.

How is academic procrastination different from, say, chronic, everyday procrastination? Academic procrastination is situation-specific. Although many students report that they engage in procrastination when it comes to schoolwork, they usually don't delay the fun activities they want to do. The college student may put off studying or reading a chapter or writing a paper until the deadline or just afterward. Yet the situation would be different if any of the following were to occur:

- There was a hip-hop concert that night.
- There was a keg of beer in a nearby fraternity house.
- There was a free movie for the first twenty students to arrive.

So, college students put off certain tasks, those that are academically related, but they don't delay fun activities with friends. Hence, this form of delay I label *situational procrastination*.

We don't have to look only at college students and their academic behavior to notice situational procrastination.

For instance, many people consistently fail to pay their credit card bills on a monthly basis. They carry over the balance month after month. Beginning in 2008, the U.S. economy suffered in part because people were purchasing more than they could afford. They were overextending themselves, month after month, and the debt kept growing. These individuals might have intended to pay their bills, but the unpaid balances simply grew and grew. People skipped one month's payment, then another, and another. Before they realized, they were in a financial hole. Finally, their bills were too big, and they wondered how they could ever meet their obligations.

For many U.S. citizens, this tendency to procrastinate also extended to their home mortgages. Similar to the situation with credit cards, people failed to pay their mortgages month after month. The consequences often were foreclosure and, in worse cases, loss of the home and homelessness.

The point here is not to sadden or depress you. Instead, I want to show you that procrastination has an impact. It is very possible that many people who couldn't pay their credit card bills or their home mortgage were not chronic procrastinators—they were, however, engaging in situational procrastination. They were not paying their bills but did continue to work and meet other obligations and deadlines. Thus, these people were procrastinating, but they are not procrastinators.

Perhaps scientists decided to focus on academic procrastination as the key form of situational procrastination because of the convenience in collecting data. All of these people have gathered together in the same location (a college campus), which makes them so easy to study. My colleagues and I have students of every age in our classes, and we witness procrastination all of the time. I have long recommended to my colleagues that we go beyond student samples. Scientists need to examine situational procrastination with older adult samples. Dr. Steven Scher, of Eastern Illinois

University in Charleston, and I, for instance, found that during an average week, people delay hundreds of tasks (e.g., returning phone calls, grocery shopping, preparing for a family vacation). We should examine situational procrastination in people other than academics. We need to include "real-world" nonstudent, community-based samples of participants in our research.

Until that day, however, I will talk about one well-known and common maladaptive strategy of situational procrastination: academic procrastination. I would like to add one more thing about academic procrastination in general. I prefer to call such delays by students' *academic procrastination*, rather than *student procrastination*, because here the emphasis is on the task. If we called it *student procrastination*, the emphasis would be on the person and his or her personality. By calling it *academic procrastination*, we place the emphasis on the setting, the tasks, and the behavior. Therefore, the student delays studying but doesn't put off getting free beer or tickets for a soon-to-be-sold-out concert.

How Prevalent Is Academic Procrastination?

In the 1970s, it was reported that as many as 70 to 75 percent of college students claimed that they frequently procrastinated on academic tasks. Since the late 1990s, that rate continues. Today we know that college students' academic procrastination rates are 70 to 75 percent among men and women attending private or public universities, private select liberal arts colleges, and even open-enrollment institutions (Ferrari, Keane, Wolfe, and Beck 1998).

Think about that—most students admit they frequently delay school-related tasks. It is such a common activity for students that it seems like second-nature for them. And it doesn't matter whether they attend an Ivy League, top-tier institution or a large land-grant, public research university—most students will procrastinate in this situation.

The Impact of Procrastination on Academics and on Life

The impact of academic procrastination on how well students perform has been examined in a number of studies, and conclusions may be found in detail in Schouwenburg et al. (2004). Nevertheless, here are a few of the characteristics of student procrastinators in the United States and other countries (cf. Özer, Demir, and Ferrari 2008). For instance, it may not surprise you that academic procrastinators, compared to nonprocrastinators, earn lower English and math grades and term paper outline grades, achieve poor final term paper grades and final course grades, and have poor cumulative GPAs.

Academic procrastinators, compared to nonprocrastinators, may receive these poor grades and evaluations because:

- They take longer to return class assignments, hand in report outlines, and hand in final papers (this is true of both undergraduate and graduate students).
- They spend more hours working on projects and studying.
- They likely engage in cheating and plagiarism.
- Even if they start to work on a project, they take a long time to finish it.
- They have more incomplete homework assignments and course work.

Is it possible, you may ask, that academic procrastinators are individuals who are different from their school peers?

The characteristics of academic procrastinators, based on the research literature, are reviewed elsewhere (see Ferrari 2004) and include more than merely a fear of failure, a poor work ethic, a general lack of motivation, and disorganization. Academic procrastinators report that they do not possess the self-efficacy to succeed in school or in life, and they feel a lack of control over their academic lives and their personal lives. In addition, academic procrastinators claim they have a *high degree* of these personality attributes:

- Self-handicapping behaviors
- Guilt feelings
- State (being anxious in a specific situation, not all the time in every place), trait, and social anxieties
- Rebelliousness
- Indecision
- Irrational thinking
- Public self-consciousness
- Societal demands for perfection
- Parental criticism
- Parental performance expectations

They also claim they have a *low degree* of these personality attributes:

- Optimism
- Decisional self-confidence
- Personal self-confidence
- Self-esteem
- Life satisfaction

Education officials wondered about the personalities of academic procrastinators (Ferrari, Parker, and Ware 1992).

For instance, educators assessed the association between academic procrastination and factors related to the Myers-Briggs Personality Indicator, which was first published in 1962 and was based on Carl Jung typologies. A very popular test for people's personality types, the Myers-Briggs sorts psychological differences into four opposite pairs, or "dichotomies," resulting in sixteen possible psychological types. None of these types is "better" or "worse"; however, Briggs and Myers recognized that everyone naturally prefers one overall combination of type differences. The Myers-Briggs indicator is often used in corporate settings, school assessments, and other places where simple, straightforward information about one's personality is desired.

Contrary to popular belief, however, academic procrastination is not related to *any* Myers-Briggs typologies. Instead, academic procrastination is associated with low academic self-efficacy (the belief that one is in charge of one's own life) and a low academic locus of control (the belief that one is in control of the events surrounding one's academic life). In other words, students who engage in frequent academic procrastination do not have a specific personality type; instead, they don't believe that they can make a difference in their academic lives and that they have control over their academic success.

Taken together, the profile of procrastinators in academic situations seems overwhelmingly negative and insurmountable. You might think it assigns blame to people for not succeeding in school. Yet procrastination is the bad habit of putting off until the day after tomorrow what should have been done the day before yesterday. It doesn't have to be like this.

Instead of searching for a general, global personality possessed by the academic procrastinator, it may be more useful to explore aspects of this person's identity. It is more useful for you, as an academic procrastinator, to understand why you engage in this situational form of procrastination and how that relates to you as a person.

Therefore, let's consider the identity style of academic procrastinators who attend both public and private universities (Ferrari, Wolfe, Wesley, Schoff, and Brett 1995). It seems that academic procrastinators claim a diffuse identity style. That is, these procrastinators have a style dominated by avoidance—they work at not learning more about themselves, about their strengths or weaknesses. Their understanding of who they are is scattered and seemingly unconnected.

As noted earlier in regard to frequent and chronic procrastination, academic procrastination is cloaked in a tendency to avoid gathering or absorbing information. Yet this knowledge could help you learn more about who you are, where you are going, and what you are capable of doing to reach your full potential.

Why do some students feel this way? Dr. Gordon Flett of York University, North York, Canada, reported that academic procrastinators consider themselves impostors. They think that they don't have the skills to succeed and they have been fooling others into thinking that they are bright. Dr Flett claims that this feeling of being an impostor is common among doctoral students.

Getting into a PhD program in psychology is very competitive, especially if you seek clinical psychology training. Believe it or not, acceptance into a clinical psychology PhD program is tougher than getting into medical school or law school. The public doesn't want to see TV shows about PhD program students, though. Instead, we look for dramas and comedies about law students and medical interns.

On a more serious note, some students admitted to doctoral psychology programs might experience a sense of being impostors—"Why did they ever select me? I don't possess very strong academic skills." The interesting thing about people who think they are impostors is that even when you show them objective evidence that they *do* have the skills and the abilities, they continue to believe they are simply phonies.

Dr. Flett of York University in Toronto found that academic procrastinators claim they are impostors in the classroom (Flett 2009). Academic procrastinators might not finish their dissertations because if they do and then obtain their degrees, this proves they do have the skills, which would negate what they believe about themselves. In addition, they might now have higher expectations for themselves—or other people might. Others could say to them, "You can do it because you have a PhD." Alternatively, they don't finish their dissertations, claims Dr. Flett, because if they do *not* succeed, then they will confirm to themselves and others that they lack important abilities, that they are incompetent.

The outcome for these doctoral students is that many academic procrastinators continue in the unofficial title of ABD—All But Dissertation. They complete everything (the course work and the various internships) except their main research dissertation.

As an academic procrastinator, you can change and can succeed in school. As with most aspects of life, you control your destiny and the course your life will take. The ability to change is within you. You have the power to stop procrastinating. Many of your methods of procrastinating can be effectively addressed by various techniques to help you stop these delaying tactics. Consider the tasks and the goals you want to achieve, and focus on meeting them, one by one.

Delayed Academic Tasks

It is more useful for you to examine the type of tasks that you delay and that make you want to procrastinate, instead of looking for personality factors that cannot be changed.

Maybe some students delay working on subjects or assignments that they perceive to be unrelated to their major. Why work on the general education classes, which don't seem directly important to their career goals?

Along with Dr. Steve Scher of Eastern Illinois University, I examined the tasks that male and female students delayed each day during a week's worth of college activities, as noted earlier in this chapter (Ferrari and Scher 2000). Students listed more than seven hundred tasks, and they indicated that nonacademic tasks were more often completed than were academic tasks, regardless of the deadline or the time frame. Tasks that students procrastinated on early in the term were reported as those requiring more effort and being more anxiety provoking and unpleasurable than any other tasks during the term. In short, to heighten the likelihood that tasks will be completed by students, both academic and nonacademic tasks should be challenging, yet fun.

You procrastinate with your schoolwork because you perceive the work to be no fun, not engaging, not worthwhile. Granted, some of the work is dull, but it may be necessary as a foundation for the next assignment. There is a famous expression that before you can learn to ride a bike, you need to learn to walk. Before you can walk, you have to crawl. It is in the process of accomplishing assignments step by step that we grow and reach our potential. We need to get beyond our comfort level and what pleases us, in order to accomplish what we need to. Tomorrow comes every day; the weekdays come only once a week.

When Is Academic Procrastination Likely to Occur? Using Lies in College

I am not assigning blame to the students who delay academic tasks. Blame does not help people move forward to reach their potential in life. Still, as Martin Luther of the Protestant

Revolution stated earlier, for many people (such as students), "not now" becomes "never." One wonders what has happened to our educational system, when a student expects and is expected to procrastinate. It's possible that certain academic procrastinators delay and then perform poorly in school because of the class structure and the characteristics of some instructors in many Western countries' classrooms.

Procrastinators in academic settings state that they often use fraudulent excuses for why they delay completing assignments (Ferrari, Keane, Wolfe, and Beck 1998). Fraudulent excuses equal lies—phony excuses. Moreover, students from both public and private schools, with admission standards that are either highly selective or open enrollment, admit that more than 70 percent of the time when they use an excuse in college, it is a lie! That percentage applies to both men and women, and it holds true for small seminar classes or large lecture classes and for lower-division freshmen classes, as well as upper-division senior courses.

In other words, instructors need to be skeptical when students give them reasons for not studying, not handing in papers, or being absent from class. The students are, most often, lying to the professors. When they say that the printer died, so they could not print the paper that was due today; when they claim to have been sick last week, so they could not prepare for class; when they say their alarm clock did not go off and they slept through the final exam; when their kids were sick the previous week, so they were not ready to give their presentation in class today—they are lying.

It seems that more than 90 percent of the time, the instructor never asks for proof for the excuse. Instead, students are told to complete the assignment by the next class. So, the student makes up a lie to get out of an assignment that is due, and the instructor "rewards" the lie by not being strict and following up. This is a situation that is ripe for procrastination and excuse making. Students are not held accountable by instructors for meeting task deadlines.

Furthermore, students report that they use lies to get out of deadline projects more often with young, lenient female professors. If you are someone who enjoys being admired by your students ("Call me by my first name"), someone who has just joined the academic life, and you are a woman, then expect to be lied to by your students. The more a student knows the instructor, the more likely the student is to lie to that instructor. Students who have taken several of your classes and whom you may have on your research team working closely with you are most likely to lie to you.

In fact, students who used fraudulent excuses said that they experienced little, if any, guilt or regret from telling these lies (Ferrari and Beck 1998). When they were asked how they felt immediately before, right afterward, and right then, when they were telling the lie, about using the lie, academic procrastinators, compared to nonprocrastinators, reported that they felt more positive about the entire experience.

What this tells us is that you cannot rely on guilt to make yourself stop procrastinating in academic situations. And you cannot depend on your instructor to hold you accountable; many will not. It is up to you to change and to deal with your procrastination tendencies. It isn't useful to lie or to blame external forces for why you delay. Instead, look at the challenges and embrace them. Focus on what you can do now, not tomorrow or the day after, and begin the journey.

Helping Academic Procrastinators Work through Writer's Block

So many students (and even nonstudents) report that they experience writer's block: an inability to begin writing a paper or documenting a project. This fact might give you comfort: the famous English writer Charles Dickens wrote the classic story *A Christmas Carol* in only six weeks in 1843, just before the holiday sales that autumn. You might say, "He did it even without a laptop, so anyone can work at the last minute to get something done, and it, too, can be a masterpiece." But there is more to this story.

You see, the original manuscript had been rejected by the publisher and returned to Dickens. So, Dickens gift-wrapped it and gave it to a friend. It changed hands many times before it was finally picked up by a publisher and printed in the 1890s.

I wanted to make a couple of points by telling you this story. First, that waiting until the last minute did not work. Dickens worked on the story, using only a quill pen, and produced a product close to the Christmas deadline, perhaps thinking he could "work best under pressure." Yet as we noted in chapter 2, that myth is meaningless. Second, his work initially did not meet the publisher's standards. Dickens had to revise what he wrote, refining it with more active verbs and tightening up his prose. The relevant point, however, is that Dickens simply wrote. He did not let writer's block, as we call it, stop him from getting the project done. Sure, the manuscript was not perfect and it needed revision—but Dickens took action. He did it.

I've seen many suggestions on how to overcome writer's block, and many people may offer you useful advice. Here are a few tips that might help:

- Excuse #1: You've chosen a topic that is now boring to you.

  Buster: Examine whether a portion of the project might be of interest to you. Can you focus on a small part of the larger project? Talk to a tutor who can help you personalize the topic to make it more interesting.

- Excuse #2: You don't want to spend time writing about something you don't understand.

  Buster: Look, you have to do it—you've committed yourself. Find out what is expected and then locate resources to help you meet those goals.

- Excuse #3: You are anxious about writing the paper.

  Buster: Consciously focus on what you *can* accomplish. Take little steps toward writing the paper, which will encourage you to take larger steps. Don't sweat the small stuff. Focus your energy by rehearsing what you think you need to do.

- Excuse #4: You are stressed out and can't write a single word.

  Buster: Take deep breaths. Stretch, stand up, and walk around for a few minutes. If necessary, repeat over and over in your head soothing suggestions such as, "Calm down," and "Relax."

- Excuse #5: You're self-conscious about your writing talent.

  Buster: Break the task into smaller steps, make a general purpose outline, and then fill in the details. Focus on writing something down, and then, if you need to, talk about the topic with a friend or a tutor. Your first draft does not have to be perfect—that's why it is called a draft.

Time-Management Tips for Academic Procrastinators

Of course, for any advice to work, you must be open to following it—not once but often. Make it a habit to engage in these activities. Here are some effective strategies to help you better manage your time:

- *Be realistic.* Factor in the appropriate amount of time you need to do a task. If you must err, allow yourself a little more time, rather than less. By having a few extra minutes, you won't stress out over trying to get that paper done.
- *Add in extra time for running errands.* You might not be aware that the printer cartridge is low on ink. So, when you begin to print that thirty-five-page final report, the printer stops after page eighteen. Give yourself more time to get the printing finished. Don't figure on printing the report the night before it is due—try doing it two days earlier. That gives you time to buy a new cartridge.
- *Planning sets you free.* If you organize the information you need before you see your adviser, you will have a more successful mentoring session than if you simply walk in and say, "Help me choose classes." Begin by scheduling your fixed time commitments—work, classes, commutes, and so on. Then fit the other random tasks into your free periods.
- *Be flexible.* Interruptions happen—life happens. Don't schedule yourself so tightly that there isn't any wiggle room when something suddenly comes up.
- *Schedule time for fun.* The advice in this book does not preclude your having fun. You've earned it. But schedule the fun activities with a beginning and an end so that they don't pull you off track.
- *Do your most challenging work first.* Successful business-man Dale Carnegie said to do the hard things first, and the easy ones will take care of themselves. Do the dreaded tasks while you are fresh and awake, and you will likely finish them more quickly.

- *Make use of waiting time.* Jot down details of difficult concepts on note cards, and review them while you stand in line for the train or wait for the dorm laundry's washing machine to become available.
- *Be aware of your best time of day.* We all work better at some times than at others. For example, don't ask my wife anything before nine in the morning, especially if it's a Saturday. Once you figure out when your "peak periods" are, then you can work more effectively during those times.
- *Choose a regular study area.* Behavioral psychologists have long said that we can use the same setting in order to make associations with things. In other words, study in the same area all of the time and then you will associate that spot with doing your schoolwork, and you'll motivate yourself to do well. Don't make the bed your study area, because that spot should be associated with sleep.
- *Make an agreement.* Study partners are a great idea. Your partner and you can discuss the priorities ahead of time and decide who is willing to do which chores. Build flexibility into your schedule, though, in case someone needs to cancel for an emergency. The point is, find doers to work with and not folks who merely want a chat session.
- *Learn to say no.* Realize that if you don't say no to certain things, you may never reach your goals. It's okay to occasionally say no. It's also okay to be a little task-oriented sometimes, instead of people-oriented and not wanting to offend others by saying no.

I hope you see that academic procrastination is common, and such procrastinators are not the same as other forms of frequent delaying individuals described earlier in this book. Academic procrastinators (and if this is you, I'm speaking to you) need to focus on the task at hand—what they need to do *now* and begin. The problem is not going away: the assignment will still be there, the chapter still needs to be read, the paper still needs its resources. Get it done, just do it now.

Procrastination at Work

Things may come to those who wait, but only
the things left by those who hustle.

—ABRAHAM LINCOLN

I like work: it fascinates me. I can sit and look
at it for hours.

—JEROME K. JEROME, WRITER AND HUMORIST

People often ask me, "What are the implications of procrastination, specifically related to my workplace?" This chapter presents information on which employees are likely to procrastinate, how other employees (including peers and supervisors who are procrastinators) view someone who frequently delays tasks in the workplace, and what job openings procrastinators often fill.

But first, here are some statistics to ponder. A December 2005 study published in the *North Coast Business Journal* reported that more than 44 percent of executives say that their staffs are much less productive during the week before a holiday. In December and January, which are critical end-of-quarter and end-of-year project deadline seasons, 48 percent of managers report that they experience much less output from employees due to procrastination. Look at the opportunities for business success that are lost at that time of year.

On June 14, 2008, the *New York Times* reported that corporate employees are interrupted on the job so often that when all of the time was added up, it amounted to 28 percent of the average workday. The survey was conducted by Basex, a company that explores workers' efficiency at information-intensive companies (e.g., high-tech, computer-based companies). Employees reported that these interruptions are unnecessary and not urgent.

One wonders whether corporate settings are simply ripe for procrastination. You may say, "Of course, I can't get anything done on time—I have too many business interruptions. The day is over by the time I am ready to start working on things." Just like the character Robinson Crusoe, I guess you won't get things done until you have Friday!

It seems odd that procrastination has become so prevalent in the workplace. Interestingly, U.S. corporate employees have gained the equivalent of thirty-three days of vacation since 1965. Time-saving innovations such as dishwashers, vacuum cleaners, and even takeout food added those six-plus extra work weeks, in small amounts, to average U.S. workers' lives from 1965 to 2003 (according to a 2006 research report by the University of Chicago and the University of Rochester). So, what have people done with those extra days? Watched TV, most likely.

Are you still not convinced about the U.S. work ethic? Steve Greenhouse, the author of *The Big Squeeze* (Knopf, 2003), reports that productivity in America increased 60 percent since 1979. Employees in the United States work 80 hours more per year than Canadians, 120 hours more per year than the British, and an unbelievable 340 hours more than the French. That's 6 more hours per week, or more than 1 hour longer per day for U.S. employees. Even so, workplace procrastination exists among U.S. employees and workers in other nations. We need to understand the prevalence of employee procrastination.

Behavioral Economics: Paying a Price to Procrastinate

We've become accustomed to getting an instant response to everything, so much so that it has become common, rather than an unusual request, to ask for something now. Consider this situation: It's the middle of August, and you order a new fall jacket from a catalog over the phone. The sales representative asks you whether you would like that jacket shipped by next-day delivery or standard shipment, which requires five business days. Which option would you select?

Now suppose you can have that same jacket shipped to you by either standard shipping or next-day delivery, but there is no charge to you for the latter because your fall jacket was so expensive, the shipping fee will be waived. Which shipping option would you choose now?

I suspect that you would ask for the jacket to be shipped to you via next-day delivery in either case. Why? Because most people have become accustomed to getting what they want *now*, and they are willing to pay the price for such service. Still, think about it: Why does a body shop need next-day delivery of paint when it has the car in the shop for three days? Why do you mail a birthday card for someone special using overnight delivery when you know that the date of the birthday is the same every year?

In my field, it's common knowledge that psychology doctoral school applications are due in December or early January—every year, only once a year. In the fifteen years that I have worked in a doctoral program, I continue to be amazed at the flood of applications that are shipped by overnight and next-day delivery on or the day before the deadline. Why have these students waited so long to send their applications when the deadline was posted well in advance?

I think the answer is that we have become accustomed to paying the price for procrastination. Next-day service has a high cost, and we are willing to pay for it. In today's e-commerce world, same-day shipping has become a normal expectation. Yet I suspect that the need for overnight shipping is often due to someone's procrastination. In the world of business, we have become accustomed to items arriving late; if we want them to come on time, we pay extra. Even when the shipping fee is waived, someone must pay, and that cost is imbedded in the price of the item. Procrastination has an economic impact on individuals, as well as on businesses.

How many hours are lost waiting for orders to come in? How many times each day must managers find busy work to occupy their shift workers because an order has not arrived? How many employees leave their jobs because they can't plan their lives around such erratic schedules, especially when they have kids to pick up after school or child-care needs they can't arrange for? These costs are passed on to all of us, through the supply chain, because procrastination has led to delays in shipments.

Professor David Laibon, a Harvard economics professor, pays his coauthors $500 if he does not deliver a promised paper or a finished product by its due date. He and other behavioral economic researchers focus on the economic decisions we make and why many people delay acting on these decisions. From an economic perspective, humans are "naturally" procrastinators because they operate with inherent impulsivity. More specifically, these researchers believe that we delay because of the way we perceive the rewards and the costs of meeting deadlines versus delaying tasks. Rewards and costs have only half the weight tomorrow that they have today. In other words, unpleasant chores feel only half as bad when we imagine doing them tomorrow, versus actually doing them today.

What a fascinating perspective! Of course, when tomorrow arrives, it becomes today. And, in turn, that task's 50 percent unpleasantness, when it would not occur until tomorrow, now becomes 100 percent unpleasantness, because it is now today. And so we delay again.

How can we break this cycle? The economic answer: put a price on it. By setting up contingencies, or consequences, for not meeting the deadline—as does Professor Laibon, who pays others $500—you may prompt yourself to get things done. Remember: be sure to follow through on the agreement.

One more example of the price of procrastination comes from a February 4, 2010, article written by Walter Updegrave, a senior editor of *Money* magazine. In the article, Updegrave notes that every time someone fails to either open or add to their 401(k) retirement fund they are losing money. For example, if someone 34 years old opens a 401(k), at an average rate of 7 percent annual return, he or she would end up with a retirement nest egg of $680,000. That amount sounds good, but it is not enough for a comfortable lifestyle in 2041 dollars. There is a price for procrastination; if only the person started saving in his or her twenties, the nest egg would have been much bigger.

If you wait to open your 401(k) when you are 40 years old, you end up with about $475,000, or 30 percent less than what you would have had by starting at age 34. The price of procrastination for the 40-year-old person is $250,000. If you wait to start that 401(k) until you are 45 years old, you end up with roughly $335,000, less than half of what you would have had if you had started in your mid thirties. Now, the price of procrastination would be $345,000. You see, failing to save money because you procrastinate is costing you money.

The Demographics of Employee Procrastinators

Who claims to procrastinate more, white-collar or blue-collar employees? White-collar professionals are women and men who may be corporate employees, education specialists, and other professionals such as doctors, nurses, or lawyers.

Most blue-collar manual workers are self-employed as truck drivers, carpenters, plumbers, and other tradespeople. It's possible that blue-collar workers do not advance in life because they are likely to take time off and delay finishing a project. Alternatively, perhaps self-employed manual workers procrastinate less because they can't afford not to work—no work means no money, which equals no livelihood. On the other hand, maybe white-collar employees procrastinate more than blue-collar workers do because they claim that they need to multitask for their jobs.

I surveyed several hundred men and women who attended public presentations on procrastination held in the Northeast and Midwest sections of the United States. Based on those surveys, DePaul doctoral student Corey Hammer and I found that white-collar employees procrastinate on the job more than blue-collar workers do (Hammer and Ferrari 2002). Among the white-collar workers, around 18 to 20 percent identify as procrastinators. Notice that these high rates of procrastinators are similar to the rates I mentioned about the global prevalence of procrastination.

It should also be noted that these high rates for white-collar workers apply to both men and women. Maybe the U.S. corporate employee needs to take a lesson from Continental Airlines. Its marketing slogan is short and simple: "Work Hard. Fly Right." If we work hard and stay focused, we will reach our distant goals and fly right.

Business managers need to consider the amount of time that their employees are not productive. Think of all of the lost, buried opportunities from unproductive workers. Maybe you see yourself here, and it may well be that you are working in irrelevant tasks. I am not assigning blame. Instead, consider what is going on in your corporate setting that promotes or facilitates your delaying tasks.

In fact, different rates of procrastination are reported by various types of white-collar workers, living in regions all across the United States (Ferrari, Dovosko, and Joseph 2005). Among corporate and noncorporate professionals, procrastination tendencies on the job are reported to be higher by corporate employees. Within various samples of U.S. corporate employees (i.e., sales employees compared to midlevel managers), there are also significant differences in reported procrastination on the job—sales employees claim to indulge in more procrastination than middle managers do. These results are the same regardless of an employee's sex.

It seems that a sizable proportion of U.S. men and women working in corporate settings are likely to engage in chronic procrastination. Why? We can only speculate, but the answer may lie with the fact that technology probably tempts us to delay working on our tasks. My statistical evidence and your personal anecdotal experience seem to suggest that the same technological tools that led to improved workplace productivity may also be counterproductive, if overused. Folks may be easily distracted by all of the high-tech gadgets that surround them.

Corporate employees believe that their cell phones, PDAs, e-mail, and fax machines give them more opportunities to procrastinate. Among young adults ages eighteen to twenty-nine years old, 41 percent said that they don't pay their bills on time every month. This fact comes from a May 2008 joint report released by Princeton Research, the National Foundation for Credit Counseling, and *MSN Money*. This fact becomes more impressive considering that all of this bill paying could be done automatically, online. Notice that in this case, technology does not seem to make people less likely to procrastinate.

The need to wait for others to respond and contribute information may also delay the next person in the production line. Whatever the reason, your procrastination at work may reflect the type of occupation you hold.

Procrastination in the workplace, however, does not seem to be limited to one geographic area more than another. Yet there are significant differences in the rates of procrastination depending on where you live in the United States, as I found in a study with DePaul undergraduates Ewa Dovosko and Nancy Joseph (Ferrari, Dovosko, and Joseph 2005). Among business managers living in the northeastern, southeastern, northwestern, or southwestern sections of the United States, those from the Northwest (specifically, Seattle and Portland) self-identify more as procrastinators than do managers from the other regions.

Therefore, it's possible that there are regional differences across the United States where men and women corporate employees are more likely to be procrastinators. Do they move to these areas because the lifestyle promotes procrastination? I don't know the answer, but it is curious to ponder.

Remember the study I described in detail in chapter 5 (Ferrari 1992b), which measured people's reactions to a story about a fictitious procrastinating employee named Mr. Nolan? The study found that all coworkers harshly evaluate procrastinating colleagues on the job, whether the coworkers are men or women, procrastinators or nonprocrastinators, bosses or peers.

Yet despite coworkers' negative feelings about procrastinators and the fact that one person's delaying tactics can affect the efficiency of an entire company, there seems to be a prevalence of procrastination in the workplace.

Nevertheless, there still does not seem to be a "safe haven" where you can work that promotes or facilitates procrastination as a lifestyle. No matter where you live, you will suffer the consequences if you continue to procrastinate in your occupation. It is time for you to change your lifestyle.

Jobs Chosen by Procrastinators: The Role of Creativity

Are some procrastinators drawn to certain occupations? When media relations and news reporters interview me and my colleagues, they often say that they can personally identify with procrastination tendencies that are motivated by a need to experience the thrill of working against the deadline. They like to wait until the last minute to interview experts, write their stories, and submit their final products to editors at midnight of the deadline.

Are reporters, for instance, more likely to be procrastinators than people working in other occupations? My colleague Dr. Piers Steel and I recently collected more than forty-three hundred online procrastination surveys filled out by adult men and women employed in more than seventy-five different occupations. Within this large sample of surveys, people who identified themselves as "news reporters" did in fact report higher levels of arousal procrastination than other corporate employees did.

Yet the question remains, do procrastinators enter the field of broadcasting or do the broadcasting media produce the procrastinators? I don't know the answer, but I do notice that certain professions seem to consist of people who are habitual, chronic procrastinators.

What would happen if news reporters submit their stories to their editors early? Would the stories be bumped up to the lead story or page one of the newspaper? Most likely, no. There is probably no incentive to get that story into the newsroom early. To help people who have difficulty meeting deadlines for work assignments, I suggest that employers give them incentives for doing tasks before the deadline. Employers need to acknowledge the fact that employees completed their tasks ahead of schedule.

How to Step Up Your Game at Work

What else can you do to avoid procrastinating in the workplace? The business world tells us to get focused in order to reap the greatest rewards. Consider these four techniques:

- *Confidence.* Rate yourself, from 1 (not at all) to 10 (totally), on the level of confidence you feel regarding your career. An honest answer to this question will help you focus on where you are and where you want to go.
- *Focus.* You may be stressed at work because you are focused on circumstances you cannot control. When you dwell on things you have no control over, you often become full of fear. With that fear will come withdrawal, regret, and procrastination. Work on maximizing your resources and skills to meet the goals you have.
- *Brand.* Maybe you need to fall in love with yourself all over again. Consider these questions: What is your brand? What do you love to do? What type of person are you? What are your passions? What bruises or hurts you? As you answer, you may shift attention to what you offer others and gravitate toward the things you can control in your life.
- *Reward.* Now you are being resourceful and are refocusing on yourself. You are excited about what it would mean to share your gifts and talents with the world. You can now (as they say in business) share your brand with the world.

Perhaps, by meeting these general goals, you can become more productive and excited about getting tasks done at work.

Here's one more thing to remember about workplace procrastination. We occasionally hear some people claim that procrastination helps them be more creative. It takes time to think about an issue or a plan of attack. You may say that you need to go slowly and procrastinate because it lets you consider alternatives, gather information, and collect your thoughts. I agree—but only to a point.

As discussed in chapter 3, it is useful to sometimes wait to gather more information before making a decision or performing an action. But if you merely keep gathering information, you are not being creative until you begin to make sense out of the information and apply it to your project. If, however, you shift to something else before you take the extra steps to bring the work to completion, your delays were not adaptive—that is, they did not help you finish the task.

Creativity may require time (i.e., procrastination) before a task may be finished (Cohen and Ferrari 2010). There may be a necessary link between having more time and producing better products. For both men and women, however, the link between adaptive creative processes and procrastination is weak at best. In other words, procrastinators really don't use that extra time for creative reflection. Instead, they merely delay their work on finishing a task.

In regard to workplace procrastination, when employees state that they need more time to be creative or productive, managers should step back and determine whether the employees' claim is valid. Managers should consider whether a particular employee's delays were driven by creativity in the past. Did this person usually come up with a better product by waiting? If he didn't (which is most likely with people who frequently delay), then managers need to consider whether to accept the claim "I need more creative time." Managers need to hold employees to deadlines but should reward them if they produce a finished product even ten minutes before the deadline.

Workplace procrastination is just not an adaptive technique, so what can be done? On a simple level, maybe you think you merely need to change the time when you work. A report in the *US Press* (May 2008) of 150 senior executives from a thousand of the largest U.S. companies reported in surveys conducted in 2005, 2002, 1998, and 1987 that productivity of employees varies by the day of the week. Don't expect much work to be done on Mondays: only 12 percent of the week's productivity occurs on that day. Similar rates can be expected on Wednesday (11 percent) and Thursday (11 percent). What about Friday? Only 3 percent of the week's total production or work product happens on the last day of the business week.

What is the most productive day? Tuesday! These reports state that 57 percent of company productivity occurs on Tuesday. "TGI Tuesday" should be our national slogan. The problem of lost productivity in companies is compounded when one considers the loss in revenue. You might think great, then next Tuesday I will be productive. Sorry, life is not that simple, because during the other days of the week, we all need to get things done. Remember, Robinson Crusoe and his man Friday, who did all of the work for Crusoe.

On the other hand, maybe you blame your tendency to delay on technology. In an eight-month internal study (reported in July 2008), the chip maker Intel found that some employees who were encouraged to limit digital interruptions (such as responding to e-mail or searching the Web) were more productive and creative as a result of their self-imposed discipline.

To address technology influences, you might

- Purchase software with back-ups, tech support, and easy-to-find files.
- Print and read an e-mail message once, then file it.
- Check your e-mail only once per hour.

- Identify very needy clients and give them more time.
- Make a decision and keep it, but develop back-up plans.

These tips are a good start. I also suggest that you identify the self-sabotaging thoughts you tell yourself as a procrastinator:

- Do you think that you work against deadlines because you are easily bored? Do you want the thrill of working against the clock? If so, then you are a procrastinator who believes he or she needs excitement to get things done. Stop living with the myth that you work best under pressure. It's irrational, and it's not productive.
- Do you try to avoid failure by never finishing or even starting tasks? Are you afraid that if you do well, you will be asked to do even more on the job, and you aren't sure that you can meet those expectations? If this sounds like you, then you are a procrastinator who avoids tasks that may reveal your strengths or weaknesses.

Knowing the pattern of your procrastination is a start toward self-improvement. There is no blame here and no excuse either. It's time to stop procrastinating and start getting things done—now.

Techniques to Help You Seize the Day

Sooner or later, you will need to get moving in the workplace, whether you are seeking a job or continuing at the present work site. And sooner, rather than later, you will need to work with others. Try this plan, suggested by business experts:

- *Recognize the differences between tasks you must do and those you want to do.* Ask yourself a series of simple, direct questions and answer them honestly. What worked last year to help the company? What will work this year to advance the company? Write down your answers; don't rely on your memory. Keep a master plan. Separate the to-do list into "Will do in 2012" and "Will not do in 2012."

- *Prioritize tasks.* Don't get caught up in the small details; focus on the big picture and move on. Make a decision. Don't avoid the possibility of failure—instead, advance toward the opportunity of success. Once you make a decision, take action. Set a deadline and stick to it.

- *Distinguish between what the team considers essential and what can wait.* Have the team participate in these decisions and make a contribution.

- *Recognize trends of the future.* Today, it is essential for a business to cultivate relationships because the old ways of advertising to create new opportunities simply are not adequate. Use technology to grow, and use your networks to build contacts. Don't forget existing relationships, but find common bonds with new clients and build on them. You can't sit and wait or hope and pray that someone comes through the door to buy your product. You must be active and must establish connections. If each member of your team brings in two new contacts through his or her network systems, imagine the new opportunities for growth.

- *Maintain social ties within and outside the company.* Celebrate the success of your team members, and remember to keep your clients' important milestone events on a handy list. Write down what is important to the clients. Then, as those events or dates approach, contact the clients. Don't try to sell them anything, but build the relationships. Don't wait for clients to come to you—"reach out and touch someone."

- *Minimize interruptions and distractions.* How many times a day do you get interrupted? Figure out ways to reduce those distractions. Maximize your day. If possible, have someone else make some of the phone calls that would waste your time. Try shutting your door, and if people don't get the message, hang a "Do Not Disturb" sign on the doorknob. Don't be antisocial, but consider the tasks that you must get done.
- *Maximize organization.* Look at your workplace—is it well organized or a mess? Clear away clutter. As I noted earlier, people spend huge amounts of time trying to find things they misplaced. Modern technological gadgets can be useful if they help you get organized and become more productive. Reduce your stress by getting more out of your workday.

Here are a few more suggestions for dealing with workplace procrastination that I have heard folks in business settings mention:

- *Figure out what is causing you to procrastinate to find a solution; you need to know what is motivating your tendency to delay.* Does fear of failure or success make you avoid beginning or finishing a task? Or are you hooked on the adrenaline rush of trying to beat a deadline because you are easily bored?
- *Conquer your fears.* You may delay turning in a report at work because you're afraid of the outcome: What if the boss doesn't like my report? What if the proposal doesn't meet the needs of the client? What if they do like this report and then ask me to take on the needs of a bigger client? Try to put the results you expect from your completed task in perspective.

- *Make a list of what needs to get done, and then organize a plan to complete each step.* Break the task down into little pieces; each smaller project is more manageable than the entire task.
- *Why not do the worst tasks first?* Psychologists have demonstrated that if we do the tasks we don't like first, the fun tasks are easier to handle—and we have something to look forward to.
- *Set realistic goals for what you need to accomplish.* Keep your goals measurable, and set them within a specific time frame. Then commit to meeting each step in the list of goals, and be sure to reward yourself as you accomplish each step—with a bigger reward for the whole project.

Workplace Task-Management Tips

The workplace is a setting where you spend much of your time as an adult. So, you need to focus on what works for you and what doesn't, in order to be productive and not procrastinate. Other people don't really like procrastinators, even if they themselves are procrastinators. Certain occupations promote opportunities to increase procrastination, but you can learn ways to better manage the tasks.

I don't believe we can manage our time—instead, we must manage our lives and the tasks we are responsible for. With that in mind, let me offer you twelve management techniques that should help you reduce workplace procrastination. These strategies are not new, and you may find them in other places, but they are worth repeating:

- *Keep a to-do list.* Include urgent and not-so-urgent tasks, and be sure to update this list often. Carry the list with you, along with a pen—this way you can add or delete tasks as you go along.

- *Allocate time.* All jobs have "crunch periods" when certain things must get done. Recognize them and give yourself enough time each day, each week, and each month to work on pressing issues.
- *Set and respect deadlines.* Are your deadlines realistic and obtainable? Create an action plan, and stick to it.
- *Use your time wisely.* Do you really need to check your e-mail every ten to fifteen minutes? Can't you set aside a morning, midday, and afternoon block of time just for e-mail? Don't open an e-mail unless you have time to read it and respond. That's tough, I know, but it's a good use of your time.
- *Stay on task.* Sure, others will have requests for you to fulfill—you may come back from a meeting and your previously empty in-box is now overflowing. But stay the course, stay on target, and stay on task about what you must do.
- *Collaborate and cooperate.* Earlier, I noted that you need to respect the time of your peers. Your colleagues will expect you to meet a deadline and finish a task that helps them move forward. We are social animals who live with others—we must work collaboratively and cooperatively.
- *Avoid unnecessary follow-ups.* Do you really need to phone or e-mail someone at 2:30 in the afternoon who promised to get you that document before the end of the business day? The person knows he or she needs to meet the deadline. Sending several reminders may annoy the individual and make him or her reluctant to meet your deadline. Stay focused, but stay cool.
- *Cancel routine meetings.* Is that weekly meeting really necessary? Can you get away with a biweekly but longer

meeting? My team meets every other Wednesday, but we meet for ninety minutes. My colleagues have weekly meetings of sixty minutes. I choose longer, less frequent meetings to give my team members time to accomplish their tasks between sessions. If you must have a meeting, do prep work beforehand to ensure an effective meeting; send out materials in advance— make sure everyone reads them. Use the meeting as a time to focus solely on the task at hand.

- *Pick your projects carefully.* Do you really need to have all of the big clients? Can't you focus on a few key ones so that you can manage their needs most effectively? The boss will be more impressed with quality than with quantity.
- *Keep busy.* Stay on top of the latest trends in your business. Keep your skills sharp, because it gives you an opportunity to switch gears and concentrate on something else for a change of pace.
- *Don't put off layoffs.* Unfortunately, in the world of work, some employees need to be terminated. If you have to make employee cuts, simply get on with it. Procrastination isn't good for anyone in this situation.
- *Enforce punctuality.* I had an economics professor in college who would lock the class door two minutes after his classes started, to show students that punctuality was valued in the workplace. Trust me, students never arrived late to class a second time.

These are suggestions that I think can work, but you must want to change.

12

Procrastination and Personality Styles

Procrastination is one of the most common
and deadliest of diseases, and its toll on
success and happiness is heavy.

—DR. WAYNE DYER, SELF-HELP AND
MOTIVATIONAL SPEAKER

―――――――

The really happy people are those who have
broken the chains of procrastination, those
who find satisfaction in doing the job at hand.
They're full of eagerness, zest, productivity.
You can be, too.

—DR. NORMAN VINCENT PEALE

There is a stark difference in the two quotes that opened this chapter. The first one seems rather negative, condemning, and condescending. Here, procrastination is portrayed as a disease, so there is little one can do to change oneself. When people have cancer, for instance, they may not be able to change their condition. Perhaps they can only treat the illness. It may not be their fault that they are condemned to suffer from the disease.

The second quote, in contrast, is more optimistic and hopeful. Now procrastination is considered to be a bad habit that people can break, a behavior they can learn to stop. And if they stop procrastinating, this leads to happiness. Although the first quote may be accurate, in that procrastination is common and hinders people's ability to be successful and happy, the second quote tells us we can change and can live productive, zestful lives.

Many clinical psychologists and professionals in the helping occupations consider chronic, frequent procrastination to be a major symptom of many psychiatric disorders. Fortunately, my colleagues and I conducted studies to explore the components of people's tendencies to frequently delay versus healthier habits of successful living (cf. Diaz-Morales, Cohen, and Ferrari 2008). Here are several lines of research we engaged in.

Procrastination and Impulsivity

People who procrastinate seem to be trying to seek accuracy and avoid speed. On the other hand, impulsive people seek speed and avoid accuracy. Psychologists call these speed-accuracy tradeoffs. We tend to sacrifice either accuracy or speed in order to gain accuracy or speed.

Procrastinators may want to be accurate (perhaps reflecting a desire to achieve perfection, as discussed in chapter 5), even at the expense of finishing a task in a timely manner. In contrast, impulsive people focus on getting things done now, quickly, in haste. They are less concerned with being right or accurate. In short, procrastination and impulsivity seem to be opposite tendencies.

If this model were true, one would expect procrastinators to be slow at finishing tasks because they want to achieve a high level of accuracy in their work. In a study (Ferrari 1993), I examined the relationship between speed-accuracy tradeoffs and procrastination, to ascertain whether delaying tasks was the opposite of impulsivity. The results were interesting, because I discovered that impulsivity and procrastination are not opposites. The more that people reported that they procrastinated, the more they also claimed to possess dysfunctional impulsivity. In other words, by procrastinating, the individuals said that they became impulsive—at the last minute. There was not enough time to perform well on the task to achieve a high degree of accuracy, so they rushed at the last minute and, as a result, performed poorly on the task.

Dr. Piers Steel from the University of Calgary reviewed the literature on procrastination, and his analysis indicates that impulsivity is indeed an aspect of procrastination (Steel 2007). Procrastinators do not engage in planning strategies to help them accomplish tasks. They think they have lots of time left to do the task, a concept called the *planning fallacy*. Dr. Tim Pychyl and students Richard Morin and Brian Salmon, all from Carleton University, Ottawa, examined the link between procrastination and the planning fallacy (Pychyl, Morin, and

Salmon 2000), the tendency to optimistically estimate time to complete a task based on past judgments about similar tasks.

They found that procrastinators, compared to nonprocrastinators, failed to meet deadlines that were imposed on them by others. In fact, they knew that the deadline was coming, and they planned to start at the last minute. They seemed to want to act dysfunctionally and impulsively.

When you procrastinate, you become impulsive right before the task is due. You purchase gifts that a friend may not really want for Christmas because you rush at the last minute to get something. You write a term paper that barely meets the minimal requirements, without researching all of the necessary references to produce an A+ report. You pull together whatever construction crew you can find to do some needed home repairs, because you did not completely search through all of the licensed contractors who were available before the roof began to leak.

Procrastination and impulsivity are not opposites. They may instead be two sides of the same coin—and they result in people not enjoying life fully, completely, happily.

Procrastination and Self-Defeating Behavior

In chapter 4, I noted that procrastination is a self-handicapping behavior, and that procrastinators self-handicap. Self-handicapping tendencies are self-defeating. They don't enable people to reach the goals they want to attain. They impede people from having successful, happy, productive lives.

The link between procrastination and personality was established with self-handicapping behaviors (Ferrari 1991a). Yet it might be useful to identify whether procrastination is related to self-defeating behaviors in general. Besides using self-handicapping tendencies as a way to defeat success, what other self-sabotaging behaviors do procrastinators use?

In reality, procrastination is related to a number of self-defeating behaviors (Ferrari 1994), namely, choosing disappointment in life, rejecting the help of others when it's needed, feeling guilty after unexpected positive events occur, rejecting participation in pleasurable situations, criticizing others and circumstances when failure occurs, rejecting others when positive events happen, and excessive self-sacrificing for others.

One wonders how engaging in any of these self-defeating behaviors might make a procrastinator more likable. Remember, procrastinators want others to like them; they are driven by the need for social approval from others. So, why, then, engage in self-defeating behaviors that are counterproductive to making oneself liked?

Moreover, procrastinating tendencies prevent people from achieving happiness and success in life. No one is blaming you for this outcome. Instead, I want to show you that procrastination is not simply an inability to manage time. Your procrastination is hindering your happiness in a number of ways. Get started, so that you can enjoy yourself more and get on with your life. Start by doing small things related to the target task. Research studies show that you will experience joy and satisfaction even from completing a portion of the task (Sheldon 2004).

Procrastination and Obsessive-Compulsive Tendencies

Many clinical psychologists and therapists state that a benchmark characteristic of obsessive-compulsive disorder (OCD) is procrastination. OCD is a syndrome that blends cognitive

processes with behavioral tendencies. People with OCD tendencies have reoccurring thoughts (obsession) and engage in
repetitive actions (compulsions). It should be noted that these
individuals don't merely think about something over and over
again. They *always* seem to be thinking about that issue—it's
an obsession that they dwell on. People with OCD are not
driven by perfectionism, by a need to do a certain task over
and over until it's perfect. Instead, they experience exagger-
ated fear that compels them to do something. Although these
habits are separate, they often accompany each other to form
the OCD category.

One may ask whether OCD traits are truly reflective
of procrastinators. The role of procrastination and obsessions and compulsions has been examined previously (Ferrari
and McCown 1994). Remember, obsessions are repetitive
thoughts—a person ruminates over and over about the same
object, person, or event. Compulsions are repetitive actions—
a person does the same act over and over. OCD individuals
have both of these cognitive and behavioral tendencies, but it
is possible to be only obsessive or compulsive.

Compulsions, but not obsessions, are related to procrastination. With clinically diagnosed OCD clients and their families,
however, the clients report higher rates of procrastination than
their immediate family members do. Adults diagnosed with
OCD report higher levels of procrastination than even the
general adult population.

Yet it is important to note that the link between procrastination and OCD was shown in clinically diagnosed
samples. This does *not* mean that you, as a procrastinator,
have OCD. I am not implying this. Instead, I suggest that you
ask yourself how adaptive and helpful your repetitive actions
are, if they hinder you from reaching your goals. Are you
happy ruminating about everything? Worry will not lead to

happiness. It will wear you down and even make you susceptible to illness.

You can stop your procrastination. You can break the chain
of dwelling on your failures and losses. Instead, savor the good
times. You can overcome your habit of performing repetitive
actions or of remaining stuck in inertia—instead, finish your
tasks and duties now and enjoy life more.

Procrastination and Attention Deficit Disorder

This is another common notion that people often have
about procrastination. It is estimated that approximately
3 to 5 percent of adults have *attention deficit disorder* (ADD).
It is manifested by inattentiveness, difficulty in getting
work done, organizational problems—and procrastination.
Approximately one-half to two-thirds of children affected
by ADD will carry it into adulthood, affecting their jobs, families, and relationships.

If ADD is untreated, the person may seem disorganized
and may rely on illegal drugs or alcohol to get by. Adults with
ADD have a sense of underachievement or of not being able
to meet their needs. They have trouble beginning tasks or following through with them. Thus, many people believe that
procrastination is associated with ADD. People with attention
deficit disorder struggle to stay focused on one thing. They multitask not out of choice, but because they can't seem to focus their
attention on one task or situation for an extended time.

Is the ADD-procrastination link supported by science or
simply a popular myth? You may believe that you have ADD
in an attempt to blame your problems on something other
than your unwillingness to change. Don't make excuses for not

dealing with your issues. I believe that attention is a skill that can be strengthened with practice.

The link does exist between attention deficit disorder with hyperactivity and frequent, chronic procrastination (Ferrari and Sander 2006). It exists, however, only for people diagnosed with ADHD. Like obsessive-compulsive disorder, ADHD combines two separate diagnoses that often go together. Someone with *attention deficit* (AD) is unable to stay focused for long periods of time, and his or her attention flits from one thing to another. *Hyperactivity disorder* (HD) is similar but has a more behavioral component. The individual moves quickly from task to task.

ADHD-diagnosed adults, when compared to a random sample of nondiagnosed, general population men and women, report themselves as persons who procrastinate often. Yet the link with procrastination should be taken with some caution, because it is based on a small sample size, which limits researchers' ability to generalize. In fact, with a larger sample of men and women drawn from individuals who were not formally diagnosed with ADHD, no relationship seems to exist between procrastination and attention deficit (Ferrari 2000). Instead, procrastination is related to a tendency to easily become bored. It is not that folks have poor attention skills; they merely seek a multitude of stimulating situations and are easily bored.

Based on these studies about attention and procrastination, it may be useful for you to consider learning or strengthening strategies and skills that keep you focused on tasks. Look at what the literature on ADD and ADHD suggests that works to keep such persons focused so they may complete tasks. Clearly, more clinical research is needed on the relation between procrastination and ADD and ADHD.

Procrastination may be a useful characteristic to explore by future researchers who are interested in clinical disorders. We need to learn whether procrastination is promoting a specific disorder, or the disorder promotes procrastination.

Before you conclude that procrastination must be a part of a disorder, consider whether you are simply unable to stay focused because you are easily bored. Do you worry about people and situations in your life, and does this worry prevent you from staying focused? For people like you, procrastination is a learned response. Your procrastination needs to be unlearned. It is not a positive lifestyle that results in happiness, to say the least. Instead, your procrastination is a function of the choices you make.

If, however, you have been diagnosed with ADD or ADHD and you find yourself procrastinating in many areas of your life, then you need coaching to help you adjust or professional assistance to teach you how to live a healthier life.

For example, making transitions from one situation to another is a challenge for people with ADHD. They have difficulty in shifting focus; this tendency is called being hyper-focused. I read about a simple technique that might help (see ADHD CoachBlog, www.additudemag.com). The author mentioned that at times, it is hard for her to get off the couch and go to bed late at night when she is tired. She focuses on the TV shows, even though she would rather go to bed and get a good night's sleep. Turning off the TV, sitting up, getting off the couch, and then walking up fourteen steps to the bedroom is a major challenge.

So, she simply places one foot on the floor while she's lying on the couch. Then, about thirty seconds later, she puts the second foot on the floor. That's an uncomfortable position, with two feet on the floor while your body remains horizontal on the couch. So she sits up. Once she is sitting, with a little more effort she stands. She focuses on the now, on getting off the couch—not on the immediate future of climbing the fourteen steps or getting to the bedroom. Slowly, one foot at a time, she walks and climbs each step. Making transitions is hard for ADHD people; focusing on a specific part of a task and doing one thing at a time might end their procrastination.

You have seen that procrastination tendencies seem to be a part of some major yet common clinical disorders. Whether your procrastination is a coping mechanism that you learned, or you have been clinically diagnosed with a disorder and procrastinating accompanies this problem, sometimes a simple solution will work in both cases. Take one step at a time, one day at a time, and stay focused on the task at hand until you overcome your tendency to delay what you need to do in life.

Where Do You Go Next—and Can You Get There from Here?

I t has been a pleasure for me to reflect on the last twenty years of studies and to see where the science of procrastination research has gone. When I seriously began to study procrastination, there was little empirical evidence on its causes and consequences. Instead, there were a few clinical observations and antidotes. A couple of self-help books were available, but they were not based on scientific fact.

Now, there have been meta-analyses of the field. Web sites exist to compile the latest scientific research. It has been a good beginning, but we need more. We still don't know whether there are any (and I suspect there are) neuro-physiological changes in the biological processes of chronic procrastinators, compared to nonprocrastinators. We need that information.

We are beginning to explore the prevalence of procrastination around the world. A few countries have collected good empirical data, but we don't know the meaning of time and procrastination in various countries and among different nationalities. We need that information.

We know that everyone delays and waits and, on occasion, procrastinates. We know that a sizable percentage of men and women use procrastination as a maladaptive lifestyle. But we don't know the impact of their lifestyle in culturally divergent settings.

We know that good cognitive-behavioral interventions exist, but we don't know how well these programs work in comparison with other programs to address the needs of chronic procrastinators. We need that information.

We need, as members of society and as social scientists, to consider the impact of procrastination on individual lives and on our nations. Clearly, there are economic, societal, ethical, and personal consequences of chronic procrastination. Let's start living lives of nonprocrastination.

A Cry for Prevention versus Procrastination

As a culture, at least within the United States, we need to change our mind-set about procrastination. It is not a laughing matter. It is a serious problem and is more likely to occur with certain people than with others. It has negative consequences that affect individual lives, yet procrastination has an even worse impact on a national scale.

In chapter 1, I mentioned that by procrastinating, we let small problems become major problems. For example, I remember reading about the need to remodel the state capitol building in Minnesota. When people first noticed that the structure was old and needed repair, perhaps a dozen years ago, it was estimated that it would cost $250,000 in state funds to remodel. The legislature decided not to invest in it at that time. Since then, the structural problems have escalated, and today it will cost more than $2 million to repair.

Prevention, not procrastination, is the message I am asking Americans to adopt. Let's postpone procrastination as a nation! Had the Minnesota legislature initially spent the money to make necessary repairs, there would be fewer costs now. This is just one example of social procrastination.

As a culture, as a society, we need to focus on getting things done. We need to have new systems to promote people's meeting deadlines. Incentives need to be created for folks to act. These need not be large incentives, but big enough to make people want to perform an act.

In 2008–2010, as you may recall, there was a global economic crisis and the economies of many nations suffered. In the United States, the federal government spent billions of dollars in bail-out funds to help large corporations and banks remain financially sound.

And then the U.S. government initiated the 2009 "cash for clunker" campaign to encourage people with older, gas-guzzling cars to trade them in to dealers and purchase new, more fuel-efficient cars. The federal government offered customers $3,500 to $4,500. Initially, the government set aside $1 billion for this program. Within a couple of weeks, the money had been spent. Americans were trading in their old cars and purchasing new ones. Dealerships could not handle the flood of new customers. The government Web site for dealers to process the funds crashed due to overload.

Within two weeks, the U.S. Congress allocated another $3 billion to ensure that every citizen who wanted to trade in an older model could purchase the more fuel-efficient models with the incentives. As of late August 2009, news reporters indicated that more than 430,000 cars were cashed in and that the funds for this initiative were now gone.

What is the point of this example? Look at how only $4 billion helped stop procrastination across the nation. It not only enabled U.S. citizens to contribute to a more fuel-efficient global environment, it stimulated automobile sales and helped the automobile manufacturers rebound from economic crisis. Meanwhile, the U.S. Congress spent tens of billions of dollars to jump-start the economy and that led to only a small, slow return.

Bring government intervention down to the grass-roots level to truly make a difference. A little bit can go a long way, especially when the incentives are directed specifically to the people. Procrastination can end when we target the right sources and create national practices to help people move forward. Incentives, even small ones, can have a major impact on getting people to stop procrastinating on a societal level.

A Plan to Transform Holiday Shopping

In chapter 2, I described my research that focused on the real-world deadline of Christmas shopping. Millions of people each year celebrate this holiday by purchasing gifts and giving them to others. They prepare their houses for special meals and family gatherings. Yet if you shop in late November, such as the weekend of Thanksgiving, you might save 10 or 20 or maybe 30 percent off the regular sale price. That's a nice amount of savings, right?

Even so, if you shop a day or two before Christmas or even on Christmas Eve, that sale price drops to 60, 70, or even 80 percent off the regular price. So, why shop early? Our culture and our society promote procrastination.

I suggest that retailers reverse that strategy. Instead, offer 70 or 80 percent off in late November and issue a surcharge for items purchased just before December 25. If people want to wait to shop, that's okay—but it will cost them. Merchants will no longer reward them for waiting. Retailers will get their profits earlier, during a period of time when they most need to make money. Stores would not be crowded right before the holiday. People would be more relaxed and could focus on the festivities of the season and perhaps the spiritual meaning of the holiday.

Recently, I read that a few retailers, during the 2009 holiday season, introduced incentive cards for shoppers. That is, early in the season they offered a $10 gift card for every $50 of merchandise purchased. One store offered a promotion of $20 in savings for every $200 in spending. These types of promotions are great, but I suggest they be offered only during the first two or three weeks of the holiday season. Don't reward late shoppers with such discount practices.

If we keep the system as is, we reward last-minute shoppers. We hear reporters say again and again that the holiday season was less profitable than expected, but thank goodness for last-minute sales and after-Christmas sales. We can and must do better. We can stop or at least reduce our procrastination as a nation.

Everyone Wins by Filing Tax Returns Early

For as long as I've known, perhaps at least a century, the annual filing of personal income taxes has occurred in the United States. Adults know that April 15 requires them to file their tax returns, pay a penalty, or ask for an extension. But what if people file early—does the federal government offer any incentive if someone pays his or her tax bill early? No. Why not? I ask.

I suggest that the federal government offer an incentive so that people do not procrastinate. Instead of punishing them with a penalty for making late payments, reward them for early payments. For instance, tax filers who owe money would be asked to send their forms and pay their taxes on February 15, instead of April 15. Consequently, the taxpayer would be able to reduce his or her payment by 3 percent. If people file by March 15, they can save 2 percent off their total taxes. Offer an incentive for early payments; reward people to act early.

The federal government would receive the funds one or two months earlier. In these tough economic times, it could use the funds sooner, rather than later. The taxpayer also benefits. Taxpayers would save a little of what they owe in annual taxes.

Do you still want to wait until April 15? Fine, you can. But now at least there would be an incentive to pay early.

Final Thoughts

For years, the manufacturers of Volvo automobiles designed their television ads to tell viewers about the advantages of their cars and the safety reasons that they should buy a Volvo. In contrast, Nike shoes kept their TV ads simple and portrayed folks performing various sports in every type of situation. Nike's tagline is the classic "Just Do It." This slogan implies that the personal benefits from owning Nike shoes will come from using them. Just do it—or, as I said earlier in this book, "Just do it *now*."

I do think we need to weigh the benefits of our acts, but most of the time we also need to simply do something. We need to take action. We will learn the benefits, experience the pleasures, and come face-to-face with our challenges and failures, but we must *do it*.

Procrastination is more than ineffective time management. It is a strategic technique that people use to ineffectively cope with life. But life is what you make it—and you can make it so much more enjoyable. There is more to life than being anxious over tasks you have to do or did not do on time. Focus on the blessings you have—family, friends, good health, pets—and go from there. You can stop procrastinating, by doing.

The problem of procrastination in our society will change only when we gather enough reliable and valid empirical facts through science, and when men and women take the topic seriously. Societal support for procrastination must stop. Lives are on the line. You and I can start; together we can change our behavior from procrastination to prevention and productivity. I look forward to the day when I can write a book that surveys the end of procrastination as we knew it.

Thank you for not procrastinating in reading this book—and thank you for doing it *now*.

References

Books

Baumeister, R. F. 1991. *Escaping the self: Alcoholism, spirituality, masochism, and other flights from the burden of selfhood.* New York: Harper Collins/Basic Books.

Burka, J. B., and L. M. Yuen. 1983: 2008. *Procrastination: Why you do it and what to do about it.* Reading, PA: Addison-Wesley.

Ettus, S. 2008. *The experts' guide to doing things faster.* New York: Clarkson Potter.

Ferrari, J. R. 1993b. Procrastination and impulsiveness: Two sides of a coin? In W. McCown, M. B. Shure, and J. Johnson, eds., *The impulsive client: Theory, research, and treatment,* pp. 265–276. Washington, DC: American Psychological Association.

———. 2001. Getting things done on time: Conquering procrastination. In C. R. Snyder, ed., *Coping and copers: Adaptive processes and people,* pp. 30–46. New York: Oxford University Press.

———. 2004. Trait procrastination in academic settings: An overview of students who engage in task delays. In H. C. Schouwenburg, C. Lay, T. A. Pychyl, and J. R. Ferrari, eds., *Counseling the procrastinator in academic settings,* pp. 19–28. Washington, DC: American Psychological Association.

———. 2010. Chronic procrastination: Life beyond ineffective time management. In F. Columbus, ed., *Time management*, pp. 147–162. Hauppauge, NY: Nova Science Publishers, Inc.

Ferrari, J. R., J. L. Johnson, and W. G. McCown. 1995. *Procrastination and task avoidance: Theory, research, and treatment.* New York: Springer Science Publications.

Ferrari, J. R., and T. A. Pychyl, eds. 2000. Procrastination: Current issues and new directions. Special issue of the *Journal of Social Behavior and Personality.* Corte Madre, CA: Select Press.

Fishbein, M., and I. Ajzen. 1975. *Belief, attitude, intention, and behavior.* Reading, MA: Addison-Wesley.

Ortberg, J. 2001. *If you want to walk on water, you've got to get out of the boat.* Grand Rapids, MI: Zondervan.

Pausch, R., and A. Zaslow. 2008. *The last lecture.* New York: Hyperion.

Schmuck, P., and K. M. Sheldon, eds. 2001. *Life goals and well-being: Towards a positive psychology of human striving.* Seattle, Toronto, Bern, Goettingen: Hogrefe and Huber Publishers.

Schouwenburg, H. C., C. Lay, T. A. Pychyl, and J. R. Ferrari, eds. 2004. *Counseling the procrastinator in academic settings.* Washington, DC: American Psychological Association.

Seligman, M. 1975. *Helplessness: On depression, development, and death.* San Francisco: W. H. Freeman.

Sheldon, K. M. 2004. *Optimal human being: An integrated multi-level perspective.* Mahwah, NJ: Erlbaum.

Snyder, C. R. (1984). *The psychology of hope: You can get there from here.* New York: Free Press.

Snyder, C. R., R. L. Higgins, and R. J. Stucky. 1983. *Excuses: Masquerades in search of grace.* New York: John Wiley and Sons.

Vanderkam, L. 2010. *168 Hours.* New York: Portfolio/Imprint.

Zuckerman, M. 1994. *Behavioral expressions and biological bases of sensation-seeking.* New York: Cambridge University Press.

Articles and Other Publications

Ajzen, I. 1988. The theory of planned behavior. *Organizational Behavior and Human Decision Processes* 50:179–211.

Ajzen, I., and M. Fishbein. 1977. Attitude-behavior relations: A theoretical analysis and review of empirical research. *Psychological Bulletin* 84:888–918.

Berzonsky, M. D., and J. R. Ferrari. 1996. Identity orientation and decisional strategies. *Personality and Individual Differences* 20:597–606.

———. 2009. A diffuse-avoidant identity processing style: Strategic avoidance or self-confusion? *Identity: An International Journal of Theory and Research* 9:1–14.

Buss, D. M. 2009. How can evolutionary psychology successfully explain personality and individual difference? *Psychological Science* 4:359–366.

Choi, J. N., and S. V. Moran. 2009. Why not procrastinate? Development and validation of a new active procrastination scale. *Journal of Social Psychology* 149:195–211.

Chu, A. H. C., and J. N. Choi. 2005. Rethinking procrastination: Positive effects of "active" procrastination behavior on attitudes and performance. *Journal of Social Psychology* 145:245–263.

Cohen, J. R. 2008. *Take some time to think it over: The relation between rumination, indecision, and divergent thinking.* Master's thesis, Department of Psychology, DePaul University, Chicago, IL.

Cohen, J. R., and J. R. Ferrari. 2010. Take some time to think this over: The relation between rumination, indecision, and creativity. *Creativity Research Journal* 22:68–73.

Diaz-Morales, J. F., J. Cohen, and J. R. Ferrari. 2008a. Indecision and avoidant procrastination: The role of morningness-eveningness and time perspective in chronic delay lifestyles. *Journal of General Psychology* 135:229–241.

———. 2008b. An integrated view of personality styles related to avoidant procrastination. *Personality and Individual Differences* 45:554–558.

Diaz-Morales, J. F., J. R. Ferrari, K. Diaz, and D. Argumendo. 2006a. Factor structure of three procrastination scales with a Spanish adult population. *European Journal of Personality Assessment* 22:132–137.

———. 2006b. Procrastination and demographic characteristics among Spanish adults: Further evidence. *The Journal of Social Psychology* 146:629–633.

Effert, B. R., and J. R. Ferrari. 1989. Decisional procrastination: Examining personality correlates. *Journal of Social Behavior and Personality* 4:151–156.

Ferrari, J. R. 1989. Reliability of academic and dispositional measures of procrastination. *Psychological Reports* 64:1057–1078.

———. 1991a. Compulsive procrastination: Some self-reported characteristics. *Psychological Reports* 68:455–458.

———. 1991b. Procrastination and project creation: Choosing easy, non-diagnostic items to avoid self-relevant information. *Journal of Social Behavior and Personality* 6:619–628.

———. 1991c. A preference for a favorable public impression by procrastination: Selecting among cognitive and social tasks. *Personality and Individual Differences* 12:1233–1237.

———. 1991d. Self-handicapping by procrastinators: Protecting social-esteem, self-esteem, or both? *Journal of Research in Personality* 25:245–261.

———. 1991e. A second look at behavioral self-handicapping among women. *Journal of Social Behavior and Personality* 6:195–206.

———. 1992a. Procrastination and perfect behavior: An exploratory factor analysis of self-presentational, self-awareness, and self-handicapping components. *Journal of Research in Personality* 26:75–84.

———. 1992b. Procrastination in the workplace: Attributions for failure among individuals with similar behavioral tendencies. *Personality and Individual Differences* 13:315–319.

———. 1992c. Psychometric validation of two procrastination inventories for adults: Arousal and avoidance measures. *Journal of Psychopathology and Behavioral Assessment* 14:97–110.

———. 1993a. Christmas and procrastination: Explaining lack of diligence at a "real-world" task deadline. *Personality and Individual Differences* 14:25–33.

———. 1994. Dysfunctional procrastination and its relationship with self-esteem, interpersonal dependency, and self-defeating behaviors. *Personality and Individual Differences* 15:673–679.

———. 2000. Procrastination and attention: Factor analysis of attention deficit, boredomness, intelligence, self-esteem and task delay frequencies. *Journal of Social Behavior and Personality* 15:185–196.

———. 2001. Procrastination as self-regulation failure of performance: Effects of cognitive load, self-awareness, and time limits on "working best under pressure." *European Journal of Personality* 15:391–406.

Ferrari, J. R., K. L. Barnes, and P. Steel. 2009. Life regrets by avoidant and arousal procrastinators: Why put off today what you will regret tomorrow? *Journal of Individual Differences* 30:163–168.

Ferrari, J. R., and B. Beck. 1998. Affective responses before and after fraudulent excuses by academic procrastinators. *Education* 118:529–537.

Ferrari, J. R., and J. F. Diaz-Morales. 2007a. Procrastination: Different time perspectives predict different motives. *Journal of Research in Personality* 41:707–714.

———. 2007b. Perceptions of self-concept and self-presentation by procrastinators: Further evidence. *Spanish Journal of Psychology* 10:91–96.

Ferrari, J. R., J. F. Diaz-Morales, J. O'Callaghan, K. Diaz, and D. Argumendo. 2007. Frequent behavioral delay tendencies by adults: International prevalence rates of chronic procrastination. *Journal of Cross-Cultural Psychology* 38:458–464.

Ferrari, J. R., and J. F. Dovidio. 1997. Some experimental assessments of indecisives: Support for a non-cognitive failures hypothesis. *Journal of Social Behavior and Personality* 12:527–538.

———. 2000. Examining behavioral processes in indecision: Decisional procrastination and decision-making style. *Journal of Research in Personality* 34:127–137.

———. 2001. Behavioral decision making strategies by indecisives. *Personality and Individual Differences* 30:1113–1123.

Ferrari, J. R., E. Dovosko, and N. Joseph. 2005. Procrastination in corporate settings: Sex, status, and geographic comparisons of arousal and avoidance types. *Individual Differences Research* 3:140–149.

Ferrari, J. R., M. Driscoll, and J. F. Diaz-Morales. 2007. Examining the self of chronic procrastinators: Actual, ought, and undesired attributes. *Individual Differences Research* 5:115–128.

Ferrari, J. R., and R. A. Emmons. (1994). Procrastination as revenge: Do people report using delays as strategy for vengeance? *Personality and Individual Differences* 15:539–544.

————. 1995. Methods of procrastination and their relation to self-control and self-reinforcement: An empirical study. *Journal of Social Behavior and Personality* 10:135–142.

Ferrari, J. R., J. S. Harriott, et al. 1997. Exploring the time preferences by procrastinators: Night or day, which is the one? *European Journal of Personality* 11:187–196.

Ferrari, J. R., J. Harriott, and M. Zimmerman. 1999. The social support networks of procrastinators: Friends or family in times of trouble? *Personality and Individual Differences* 26:321–334.

Ferrari, J. R., S. Keane, et al. 1998. The antecedents and consequences of academic excuse-making: Examining individual differences in procrastination. *Research in Higher Education* 39:199–215.

Ferrari, J. R., and M. R. Leippe. 1992. Noncompliance with persuasive appeals for a prosocial, altruistic act: Blood donating. *Journal of Applied Social Psychology* 22:83–101.

Ferrari, J. R., C. Mason, and C. Hammer. 2006. Procrastination as a predictor of task perceptions: Examining delayed and non-delayed tasks across varied deadlines. *Individual Differences Research* 4:56–64.

Ferrari, J. R., and W. McCown. 1994. Procrastination tendencies among obsessive-compulsives and their relatives. *Journal of Clinical Psychology* 50:162–167.

Ferrari, J. R., J. O'Callaghan, and I. Newbegin. 2005. Prevalence of procrastination in the United States, United Kingdom, and Australia: Arousal and avoidance delays in adults. *North American Journal of Psychology* 7:1–6.

Ferrari, J. R., and M. J. Olivette. 1993. Perceptions of parental control and the development of indecision among late adolescent females. *Adolescence* 28:963–970.

———. 1994. Parental authority influences on the development of female dysfunctional procrastination. *Journal of Research in Personality* 28:87–100.

Ferrari, J. R., B. U. Özer, and A. Demir. 2009. Chronic procrastination among Turkish adults: Exploring decisional, avoidant, and arousal styles. *Journal of Social Psychology* 149:302–307.

Ferrari, J. R., J. T. Parker, and C. B. Ware. 1992. Academic procrastination: Personality correlates with Myers-Briggs types, self-efficacy, and academic locus of control. *Journal of Social Behavior and Personality* 7:495–502.

Ferrari, J. R., and T. Patel. 2004. Social comparisons by procrastinators: Rating peers with similar and dissimilar delay tendencies. *Personality and Individual Differences* 37:1493–1501.

Ferrari, J. R., and T. A. Pychyl. 2007. Regulating speed, accuracy, and judgments by indecisives: Effects of frequent choices on self-regulation failure. *Personality and Individual Differences* 42:777–787.

———. 2008. *"Just wait . . . someone else will do it:" A five-factor theory investigation of conscientiousness in relation to procrastination and social loafing.* Unpublished manuscript.

Ferrari, J.R., and S. E. Sanders. 2006. Procrastination rates among non-clinical and clinical adults with ADHD: A pilot study. *Counseling and Clinical Psychology Journal* 3:2–9.

Ferrari, J.R., and S. J. Scher. 2000. Toward an understanding of academic and nonacademic tasks procrastinated by students: The use of daily logs. *Psychology in the Schools* 34:359–366.

Ferrari, J. R., and D. M. Tice. 2000. Procrastination as a self-handicap for men and women: A task avoidance strategy in a laboratory setting. *Journal of Research in Personality* 34:73–83.

Ferrari, J. R., R. N. Wolfe, et al. 1995. Ego-identity and academic procrastination among university students. *Journal of College Student Development* 36:361–367.

Fishbein, M. 1980. A theory of reasoned action: Some applications and implications. In H. H. Howe Jr. and M. M. Page, eds., *Nebraska Symposium on Motivation*, 1979, Vol. 27, pp. 65–116. Lincoln: University of Nebraska Press.

Flett, G. 2009: August. *Procrastination cognitions in stress and distress.* Paper presented at the 6th Biennial International Meeting on the Study and Treatment of Procrastination, York University, Toronto, Canada.

Haghbin, M., A. McCaffrey, and T. A. Pychyl. 2009. *SEM analysis of the relationship between fear of failure and procrastination.* Paper presented at the 6th Biennial International Meeting on the Study and Treatment of Procrastination. Toronto, Canada.

Hammer, C. A., and J. R. Ferrari. 2002. Differential incidence of procrastination between blue- and white-collar workers. *Current Psychology* 21:334–338.

Harriott, J., and J. R. Ferrari. 1996. Prevalence of procrastination among samples of adults. *Psychological Reports* 78:611–616.

Harriott, J., J. R. Ferrari, and J. F. Dovidio. 1996. Distractibility, daydreaming, and self-critical cognitions as determinants of indecision. *Journal of Social Behavior and Personality* 11:337–344.

Lay, C. H. 1986. At last, my research on procrastination. *Journal of Research in Personality* 20:474–495.

———. 1988. The relation of procrastination and optimism to judgments of time to complete an essay and anticipation of setbacks. *Journal of Social Behavior and Personality* 5:91–103.

———. 2009. *Moving forward in life: A guide to directed everyday living.* Paper presented at the 6th Biennial International Meeting on the Study and Treatment of Procrastination. Toronto, Canada.

Lay, C. H., and P. Burns. 1991. Intentions and behavior in studying for an examination: The role of trait procrastination and its interaction with optimism. *Journal of Social Behavior and Personality* 5:91–103.

Mann, L. 1982. Decisional procrastination scale. Items found in J. R. Ferrari et al., 1995, *Procrastination and task avoidance.* New York: Springer.

McCloskey, S., T. A. Pychyl, and J. R. Ferrari. 2009. *Perfectionism and procrastination: An exploration of their association among students.* Manuscript in preparation.

McCown, W., and J. Johnson. 1989. Adults inventory of procrastination. Items found in J. R. Ferrari et al., 1995, *Procrastination and Task Avoidance.* New York: Springer.

McCrea, S. M., N. Liberman, Y. Trope, and S. J. Sherman. 2008. Construal level and procrastination. *Psychological Science* 19:1308–1322.

Negra, A., N. Mzoughi, and O. Bouhlel. 2008. E-procrastination: A netnographic approach. *Journal of Consumer Behavior* 7:103–119.

Owens, S. G., C. G. Bowman, and C. A. Dill. 2008. Overcoming procrastination: The effects of implementation intentions. *Journal of Applied Social Psychology* 38:366–384.

Özer, B. U., A. Demir, and J. R. Ferrari. 2009. Exploring academic procrastination among Turkish students: Possible gender differences in prevalence and reasons. *Journal of Social Psychology* 149:241–257.

Perry, J. 2008. Structured procrastination. www.structuredprocras tination.com.

Pychyl, T. Procrastination Research Group. www.procrastination.ca.

Pychyl, T. A., R. W. Morin, and B. R. Salmon. (2000). Procrastination and the Planning Fallacy: An examination of the study habits of university students. *Journal of Social Behavior and Personality* 15:135–150.

Scher, S. J., and J. R. Ferrari. 2000. The recall of completed and non-completed tasks through daily logs to measure procrastination. *Journal of Social Behavior and Personality* 15:255–265.

Schouwenburg, H. C. 1992. Procrastinators and fear of failure: An exploration of reasons for procrastination. *European Journal of Personality* 6:225–236.

Simpson, W. K., and T. A. Pychyl. 2009. In search of the arousal procrastinator: Investigating the relation between procrastination, arousal-based personality traits and beliefs about procrastination motivation. *Personality and Individual Differences* 47:906–911.

Sirois, F. M. 2009. Blame it on time: A new perspective on procrastination, perfectionism, and task performance. Paper presented at the 6th Biennial International Meeting on the Study and Treatment of Procrastination. Toronto, Canada.

―――. 2007. "I'll look after my health, later": A replication and extension of the procrastination-health model with community-dwelling adults. *Personality and Individual Differences* 43:15–26.

―――. 2004. Procrastination and intentions to perform health behaviors: The role of self-efficacy and the consideration of future consequences. *Personality and Individual Differences* 37:115–128.

Sirois, F. M., M. L. Melia-Gordon, and T. A. Pychyl. 2003. "I'll look after my health, later": An investigation of procrastination and health. *Personality and Individual Differences* 35:1167–1184.

Snyder, C. R., and R. L. Higgins. 1988. Excuses: Their effective role in the negotiation of reality. *Psychological Bulletin* 103:193–210.

Solomon, L. J., and E. D. Rothblum. 1984. Academic procrastination: Frequency and cognitive-behavioral correlates. *Journal of Counseling Psychology* 31:503–509.

Specter, M. H., and J. R. Ferrari. 2000. Time orientation perceptions among procrastinators: Focusing on the past, present or future? *Journal of Social Behavior and Personality* 15:197–202.

Steel, P. 2007. The nature of procrastination: A meta-analytic and theoretical review of quintessential self-regulatory failure. *Psychological Bulletin* 133:65–94.

Sumner, E. 2009. *Procrastination, rumination, and savoring: An exploration of the cognitive underpinnings of task delay.* Unpublished master's thesis, Department of Psychology, DePaul University, Chicago, IL.

Tice, D. M., and R. F. Baumeister. 1997. Longitudinal study of procrastination, performance, stress, and health: The costs and benefits of dawdling. *Psychological Science* 8:454–458.

Wretschko, G., and P. Fridjhon. 2008. Online flow experiences, problematic Internet use and Internet procrastination. *Computers in Human Behavior* 24:2236–2254.

Index